T0135065

Smart Cities: Cyber Situational Awareness
to Support Decision Making

Nataliia Neshenko • Elias Bou-Harb • Borko Furht

Smart Cities: Cyber Situational Awareness to Support Decision Making

Springer

Nataliia Neshenko
Boca Raton, FL, USA

Elias Bou-Harb
San Antonio, TX, USA

Borko Furht
Boca Raton, FL, USA

ISBN 978-3-031-18466-6   ISBN 978-3-031-18464-2   (eBook)
https://doi.org/10.1007/978-3-031-18464-2

This Springer imprint is published by the registered company Springer Nature Switzerland AG
The registered company address is: Gewerbestrasse 11, 6330 Cham, Switzerland

Preface

The challenges in urbanization forced worldwide governments and industries to embrace the smart city vision. A modern urban infrastructure no longer operates in isolation but instead leverages the latest technologies to collect, process, and distribute aggregated knowledge to improve the quality of the provided services and promote the efficiency of resource consumption. However, this technological development manifests in the form of new vulnerabilities and a plethora of attack vectors. The ambiguity of ever-evolving cyber threats and their debilitating consequences introduce new obstacles for decision-makers. Therefore, cyber situational awareness of smart cities emerges as a mission-critical task that requires novel strategies for practical and prompt decision-making. By synthesizing the body of existing knowledge on cyber incidents, detection, and cognition methods, this book strives to advance the adoption and deployment of corresponding strategies in the realms of smart cities.

This book overviews the drivers behind the smart city vision, describes its dimensions, and introduces the reference architecture. It further enumerates and classifies threats targeting the smart city concept, links corresponding attacks, and traces the impact of these threats on operation, society, and the environment. Besides, it introduces a data-driven situational awareness, provides an in-depth description of the respective solutions, and highlights the prevalent limitations of these methods. More importantly, the book points out promising research directions and emphasizes the demand and challenges for developing holistic approaches to transition these methods to practice to equip the user with extensive knowledge regarding the detected attack instead of a sole indicator of ongoing malicious events. To this end, the book introduces a cyber situational awareness framework that can be integrated into smart city operations to provide timely evidence-based insights regarding cyber incidents and respective system responses to assist decision-making.

What Is Covered in This Book?

Our goal is to cover the topics from the motivation behind smart cities to defining its essential elements to studying cybersecurity threats and building a foundation for cyber situational awareness using data-driven methods and deep learning algorithms. This book is divided into two parts. Part I magnifies the motivation and significance of the concept of smart city (Chap. 1) and its particular challenges concerning cybersecurity (Chap. 2). Part II studies situational awareness methods that address elements of smart city technologies (Chap. 3), defines situational awareness programs, and offers the corresponding framework for ICS deployed in critical infrastructure (Chap. 4) and its particular case - water facilities (Chap. 5). Chapter 6 points out research directions and stresses the demand and challenges for developing holistic strategies and techniques to enforce cyber situational awareness methods in practice. Each chapter in the book can stand alone, defining a particular aspect of smart city or cyber situational awareness for it. There is a sequence in each chapter that builds on the previous one to provide a conceptual understanding of the smart city concept and detailed cybersecurity threats coupled with an approach for getting started with building cyber situational awareness.

Chapter 1: Rise of Smart Cities
Facing the socioeconomic challenges in urbanization, worldwide governments and industries embrace the smart city concept and establish transformation projects that demonstrate tremendous growth. These projects combine information and communication technologies to engage and integrate citizens, visitors, and business communities into an intelligent ecosystem to support better decision-making and cocreating solutions for urban issues. This engagement positively shifted essential city operations toward sustainable, effective, and efficient functions. This chapter strives to shed light on the drivers behind the concept and sets the scene for the smart city by providing its definition, separating building blocks, and highlighting contemporary technological advances.

Chapter 2: Cyber Brittleness of Smart City
This chapter shifts the focus on the cyber fragility of the smart city concept, elaborates on fundamental peculiarities of smart city cybersecurity, and raises awareness regarding past real-world cyber incidents that affected smart cities. It examines prevailing threats targeting smart cities that are identified from actual and potential cyberattacks.

Chapter 3: Cyber Situational Awareness Frontier
Cyber situational awareness or network security awareness is a vital component of a holistic view of cybersecurity. This chapter puts forward a new perspective on sustained cyber situational awareness for smart cities. It explores monitoring and attack detection methods to support the perception of cyber awareness. Further, it examines risk assessment methods and contextualized threat intelligence, which

enable the characterization and anticipation of advanced and coordinated threats via assessing their possibilities and impact. Finally, the chapter explores the strategies that model dependencies among smart cities' components to clarify how threats affect the entire ecosystem.

Chapter 4 Cyber Situational Awareness for Industrial Control Systems (ICS) Deployed in Smart City

The increased number of cyberattacks against critical infrastructure, in particular, their vulnerable network-assessable automated control systems, paved the way for new approaches to defining cyber situational awareness and forensic methods for smart cities. This chapter defines the activities required to enforce a sound situational awareness program and elaborates on design challenges that hinder the transition to operation in ICS realms. This chapter introduces a framework to integrate into operation to enhance situational awareness by providing evidence-based insights about ongoing cyber incidents and respective system responses to assist decision-making.

Chapter 5: Case Study: Situational Awareness for Water Treatment Systems

Cyberattacks on water systems can cause significant damage to the ICS equipment and render chemical or biological hazards, which can have social and financial implications. This chapter recaps the history of cyber incidents against water systems and conveys the significance of cyber situational awareness in this environment. To this end, this chapter offers a business case for applying the cyber situational awareness framework to the small-scale water treatment plant, similar to those found in small cities.

Chapter 6: Looking ahead: Future Perspectives and Opportunities of Cyber Situational Awareness for Smart City

Smart cities worldwide suffer from rapidly evolving cyber threats and attacks that exploit advanced heterogeneous technologies. Thus, failing to manage these cyber threats impairs the trustworthiness of smart cities' endeavors. Although research and operational communities are actively developing the methods to address this imperative task, numerous observations require attention. This chapter encapsulates several issues on sustained cyber situational awareness for smart cities and elaborates on several possible research directions to address these topics.

Boca Raton, FL, USA   Nataliia Neshenko
San Antonio, TX, USA   Elias Bou-Harb
Boca Raton, FL, USA   Borko Furht
January 2022

Contents

Part I
Cybersecurity of Smart City

99 *Great results can be achieved with small forces.*
— Dalai Lama

Chapter 1
Rise of Smart Cities

Facing the socio-economic challenges in urbanization, worldwide governments and industries embrace the smart city concept and establish transformation projects that demonstrate tremendous growth. These projects combine information and communication technologies to engage and integrate citizens, visitors, and business communities into an intelligent ecosystem to support better decision-making and co-creating solutions for urban issues. This engagement positively shifted essential city operations toward sustainable, effective, and efficient functions. The application of smart technologies and data harnessing methodologies developed numerous solutions to cities' key challenges (including rapid urbanization, increased home-lessness, rise in crime, climate change, and more). From improving traffic conditions to optimizing energy consumption, smart cities enhance the quality of life of their residents by reducing carbon emissions while optimizing utility costs. This chapter strives to shed light on the drivers behind the concept and sets the scene for the smart city by providing its definition, separating and elaborating on each building block, and highlighting contemporary technological advances.

This chapter first overviews the challenges of modern cities in Sect. 1.1 and sets the scene for the smart city concept in Sect. 1.2 by providing a definition and exploring its dimensions from architectural, technological, economic, and social perspectives. Finally, Sect. 1.3 concludes the chapter.

1.1 Forces of Change

Despite the global pandemic and ongoing wars, the world's population is rapidly increasing; it has almost reached 8 billion as of May 2022 [4]. With the immense growth, the world witnessed an increasing concentration of residents in the cities: more than half the world's population currently lives in urban areas (Fig. 1.1), and the trend is projected to continue. Accordingly, the United Nations predicts that two-

N. Neshenko et al., *Smart Cities: Cyber Situational Awareness to Support Decision Making*, https://doi.org/10.1007/978-3-031-18464-2_1

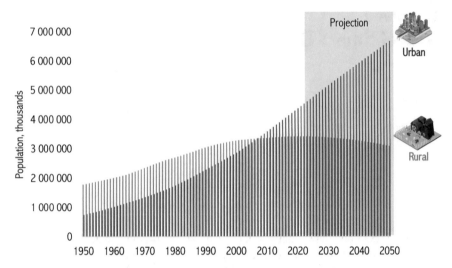

Fig. 1.1 Global urbanization, 1950–2050, thousands. Source: United Nation Department of Economic & Social Affair

Fig. 1.2 Major challenges of modern cities

thirds of the world population will live in towns and cities by 2050 [19], implying that around 1.5 million people around the globe will move into urban areas every week [22].

This unprecedented population boom will put tremendous strain on urban infrastructure and comes with a myriad of challenges and opportunities. Natural hazards, resource exhaustion, sustainability of fiscal policies, traffic congestion, safety, and citizen engagement are only a few challenges modern cities face (Fig. 1.2.)

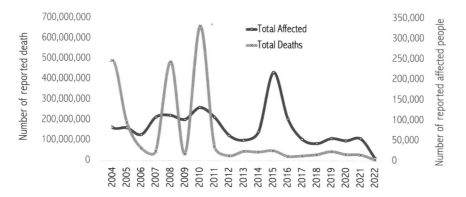

Fig. 1.3 Natural disaster summary 2004–2022

Natural Hazard

Floods, heat and cold waves, tsunamis, tropical cyclones, blizzards, and fire-storms, to name a few, affect the human population in both rural and metropolitan areas. The tremendous strain on the city's infrastructure, which emerged from the rapid growth of the urban population, coupled with severe weather events, is indeed exacerbating the devastating financial and safety impact of natural hazards. Based on data reported by the Center for Research on the Epidemiology of Disasters [9], the overall number of deaths from natural hazards declines, while the disaster-affected population is increasing or remains the same. (Note: these data do not include the pandemic effect.) (Fig. 1.3).

Making cities more resilient against these natural hazards is one of the biggest challenges faced by city leaders and demands imperative attention.

Resources Exhaustion

Cities require resources such as water, food, and energy to survive. Approximately 70–75% of total natural resources are consumed within urban areas [25]; expected population growth puts even greater stress on the urban system and affects the basic principles of sustainability. An increase in population may worsen issues with water and wastewater systems. Indeed, the infrastructure should be expanded to increase freshwater supply, which is vital for residents and for the agriculture sector. As freshwater supply cannot meet the demand, water quality can affect the well-being of the citizens. As a result, the cost of managing resources that can be supplied to citizens dramatically increases. Consequently, food and water prices may increase and create social distress, especially among the poorest residents. Beyond these basic resources, the lack of water to maintain green zones within urban areas negatively affects the livability of the metropolis.

It is crucial to address the issue of direct and indirect resource demand of cities, inevitable resource scarcity in the reality of rising demand for goods and services, and environmental impact induced by a growing population in urban systems.

Funding

Funding the infrastructure development to address ever-growing demand becomes a big challenge since the funds might not be available until after the population in urban area increases and the local government collects respective taxes. However, it is too late to mitigate the demand: building new roads and bridges, energy and water supply lines, and similar infrastructural projects are time- and capital-consuming and require funds before the population increases. On the other hand, the areas with a decreased population also struggle: they do not have sufficient capital to maintain current infrastructure and provide service to existing residents.

Therefore, the local government should find ways to fund required infrastructure development to support urbanization.

Traffic Congestion

Rapid increases in population also result in increased demand for solving basic mobility problems such as moving from one place to another at the same time: more people need to get to their workplace, and more children must get to school. The high cost of constructing and maintaining transit infrastructure leads to the absence of public transportation in many cities. Therefore, people are forced to use their own private vehicles to get places. With more people using private vehicles moving at the same time, the road system lacks the capacity to address peak-hour loads without forcing citizens to wait in line to utilize a limited road span. The lack of public transportation also limits the opportunities to support local economies, while more and more people would use it to get places faster.

Citizen Engagement

The critical aspect of living in the smart city is to connect citizens and exchange social experiences and share physical space [24]. Cities' populations have become bigger and more diverse. Therefore, leading these cities is now a more complex task than ever. As the number of metropolis habitats grows, many cities will see an increase in the number of underprivileged citizens. It is a well-known concern that different groups of urban residents can experience uneven treatment or access to essential resources, affordable technologies, and education. This inequality threatens to destabilize society and reduce benefits from urbanization.

The goals of modern governance should address the issues of livability, sustainability, and equity. It is imperative to ensure that city development results are in line with the needs of different groups of citizens and are distributed equally.

Safety

The urbanization trend and growth of megapolises complicated the communication and interaction between cities and led to a negative effect on the criminality rate [5]. Other public issues such as terrorism, insurgency in urban spaces, and vulnerable critical infrastructure increase the impact of criminal activities. Evolving trend of urban population growth forced local governments to review their approach to the safety of the cities and engage society.

These and many other challenges forced metropolitan leaders to focus on effective and efficient ways to address these emerging problems. One way to do so is to embrace digital transformation and integrate smart processes into city operations. Nowadays, city leaders think beyond the digitalization and automation of their administrative functions; they implement new technologies to deliver essential services to citizens in a new and more effective way and welcome the concept of a smart city.

1.2 Set the Scene for Smart City

There is no universal definition of a smart city exists [20]. There are, however, a number of components that are common for every city that is considered to be smart. A smart city refers to the embodiment of information and communication technologies (ICT) to promote sustainable development in urban areas. By integrating and ingesting rapid technological advances, financial, managerial, and civilized components, local governments and businesses push the adoption of digital data and intelligent analytic to achieve their goals. The latter includes but is not limited to providing better citizens' services, improving quality of life, and reducing environmental damages.

Recent research [1] indicates the global smart city market to reach US$2.51 trillion in 2025, implying a compound annual growth rate (CAGR) of 20.51% during the period from 2021 to 2025 (Fig. 1.4). Rising urbanization, demand for efficient management and resource utilization, the need for prompt and efficient transportation systems, and public safety concerns are anticipated to be the primary factors pushing the growth of the smart cities market. From improving traffic conditions to optimizing energy consumption, smart cities enhance the quality of life of their residents by reducing carbon emission while optimizing utility costs.

Fig. 1.4 Global smart city market

1.2.1 What Make City Smart?

But what makes a city smart? The city is considered smart when it uses technology to address challenges the citizens and local governments face and to scale the solutions to their maximum potential to make cities more livable. Generally, residents require cities to be citizen-centric and address their particular needs of mobility, safety, comfort, and economic efficiency. Not surprisingly, technology plays a significant role in designing solutions to meet the expectation and authorities. Therefore, any discussion of smart urban development should start with a study of infrastructure and enabling technologies.

Rising global urbanization surged infrastructural and technological investment. The world witnessed extensive development in new infrastructure to support the ever-growing large population to meet their environmental, social, and economic goals. With the embedding of latest technologies varying from telecommunication enablers to advances in data-driven artificial intelligence, Internet-connected municipal infrastructure, parking meters, and alike, continue to collect and analyze data to support decision-making and pinpoint deficiencies for real-time optimization.

Smart city infrastructure incorporates Internet of Things (IoT), communication infrastructure, cloud computing, processing components, control and operating elements, artificial intelligence (AI), big data, and more as shown in Fig. 1.5. Let us take a look at several technological advances that turn the needs and hopes of people who live in the urban area into reality.

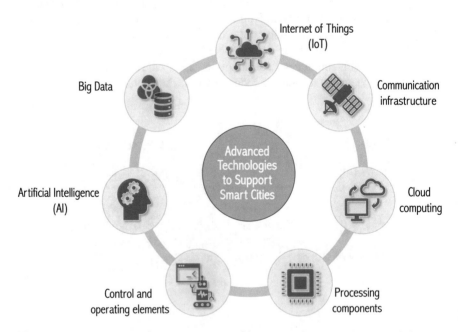

Fig. 1.5 Advanced technologies to support smart cities

IoT plays a significant role in collecting measurements from the physical environment and transmitting accumulated data to the processing units for further analysis to support the decision-making process. These resource-constrained devices can be found in various settings such as private and public companies, apartment buildings, and utility and service providers. They take many forms and materialize as diverse gadgets ranging from smartphones to wearable devices to smart meters to surveillance cameras and industrial sensors.

Communication infrastructure in form of wireless networks (WLANs), wide area networks (WANs), cellular networks, and alike plays an instrumental role in smart city. It enables data transmission and helps to connect physical and cyber worlds.

Cloud computing is on-demand access to computing resources such as virtual or physical servers, networks, analytical algorithms, computational power, development instruments, storage, applications, and alike. The main advantage of cloud computing is its scalability: the customers (e.g., local government, private and public institutions, etc.) do not require investment into equipment upfront but rather scale the required services when it is needed.

Processing components take data from cloud computing and analyze it using different data processing algorithms and provide access to information in accordance with access privileges.

Control and operating elements such as actuators operate on the results from analytical algorithms to close a feedback loop with the physical world. The elements adjust or manipulate the equipment response in order to support the efficiency and sustainability of the operation. For instance, based on the quality parameters in treated water, the response may adjust the number of chemicals to induce. Another example is a heating system: depending on the trends and overall temperature, the heating system can use energy more efficient.

Artificial intelligence (AI) refers to a complex system that incorporates various elements such as domain knowledge, human experience, procedures, computational and control units, software, data, and alike to simulate human intelligence [27]. Actually, artificial intelligence (and broadly learning methods) is among the most significant trends in the smart city markets, while privacy and cybersecurity are the biggest challenges and concerns [1]. AI is tightly coupled with big data that provide the main source of information and feedback loops for learning, reasoning, and self-correction.

Big data refers to the term used to describe the complex data collections that are hard to be processed by traditional processes due to their volume, velocity, value, variety, and veracity.

1.2.2   Dimensions of Smart City

The urban infrastructure integrates and ingests rapid technological advances such as digital data and smart analytic, which provide better services to the citizens,

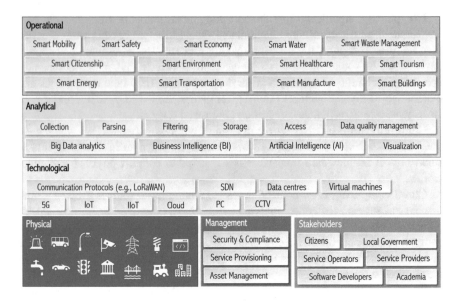

Fig. 1.6 Smart city reference architecture

improve quality of life, and reduce environmental damages. To illustrate the evolving nature of smart cities, a number of authors showcased the undertaken technological advancements while providing an overall description [10, 13, 21] and a domain-specific implementation [2, 6, 10, 23]. The main focus of these articles is to illustrate the technological advances and the importance of the interaction between social and technical systems. In fact, this interaction was revealed to be a critical role that addresses the urban challenges and supports innovation and entrepreneurship. Although the incorporation of these elements depends on the development strategy and the level of implementation in a particular city, the analysis of the implementation progress of several smart city initiatives allows modeling the reference architecture at different operational layers.

To sustain the required infrastructure, six tiers—the *physical, technological, analytical, operational, the management layer*, and the *stakeholders*—represent the smart cities architecture. Figure 1.6 gives a visual representation of a smart city's architecture along with its six layers.

1.2.2.1 Physical Tier

The *physical tier* encompasses engineered facilities, utilities, systems to address associated issues of economic growth, climate change, and municipal waste. From an engineering perspective, this tier refers to the systems that support municipal utilities such as electric, telecommunication, water, wastewater, gas, to name a few. It further includes urban streetlights, highway components, irrigation systems segments such as canals and dams, municipal buildings such as schools, hospitals, fire station, and alike.

1.2.2.2   Technological Tier

The *technological tier* is comprised of the hardware and communication technologies, which enable the collection of data from the environment and transmit it to the next architectural layer. The hardware may consist of different types of sensors, devices, or virtual machines. Various sensors are employed in the environment to collect its state. Among them are pollution, smoke, motion, brightness sensors, surveillance cameras, and energy and water meters. Additionally, various protocols, including IEEE 802.15.4, IEEE 802.15.4g, Bluetooth, LoRsa, LoRaWAN empower the sensors for data curation and harvesting so that they can deliver the information to the data layer. A plethora of researchers in academia and industry worked on actuators, sensor networks, IoT, Vehicular Ad Hoc Networks (VANETs), Mobile Ad Hoc Networks (MANETs), and access and transmission networks [10, 13, 21] to advance technological progress. For instance, transmission networks can be used to support better decision-making and resource allocation for smart grids, water and waste management, safety, emergency solutions, and much more by enabling data communication.

1.2.2.3   Analytical Tier

The *analytical tier* is the heart of smart cities. It consists of an immense volume of unstructured data that should be collected and properly stored to enable open access and the application of numerous algorithms for better decision-making. Among the most popular methods in this layer is artificial intelligence. Furthermore, one of the important functions of this tier is placing analytic into the visual context to enable the interpretation of data importance and to enhance the supervisory process. Finally, this layer takes care of the data exchange between data owners, service providers, and users by offering open data platforms.

1.2.2.4   Operational Tier

The *operational tier* represents the variety of complex solutions that smart cities provide to their customers. The application of smart technologies and data harnessing methodologies developed numerous solutions to cities' key challenges (including rapid urbanization, increased homelessness, rise in crime, climate change, and more). The smart city infrastructure comprises cyber systems integrated into physical components in various environments and includes critical infrastructure like energy, transportation, government, etc. Cities around the world offer various

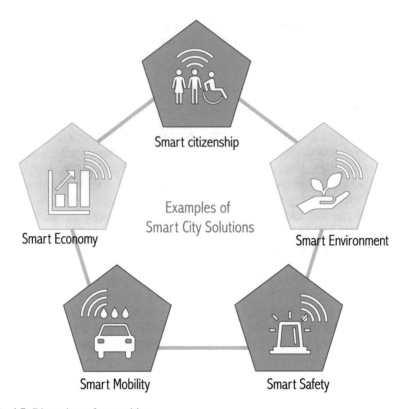

Fig. 1.7 Dimensions of smart cities

operational solutions to their citizens. These solutions and their priorities vary depending on the requirements and challenges of the specific city. The prevailing share of the global smart city market has invested in governance and education, energy and other utilities, healthcare, security, technological infrastructure, and mobility [1]. Herein are several examples of the solutions, such as smart citizenship, smart environment, smart safety, mobility, and smart economy (Fig. 1.7).

Smart Citizenship

Smart citizenship solutions offer a more inclusive society. The technology and analytical innovations are developed to improve knowledge management, provide capabilities for reaching out to the citizens, understand issues and ideas, provide access to education, and grow social capital. For instance, city administrations grant access to e-government websites to interact with public services and support the proactive position of the citizens, enhance the decision-making process, and engage citizens and businesses in co-creating solutions for urban issues [8]. This engagement positively shifted essential city operations toward sustainable, usable, and efficient functions.

Smart Environment

Comprehensive collected real-time data support the ability to monitor events as they develop, understand the changes in utilities demand patterns, and allow to deliver faster and cheaper solutions. In particular, technological innovations revise the approaches to economic infrastructure: the introduction of supported IoT devices overcomes the limitations of conventional monitoring systems. Indeed, sensors collect various environmental measurements such as air pollution levels or water chemical conditions, while intelligent platforms correlate obtained data in order to tailor warnings or to avoid ecological disasters. Additionally, intelligent building systems respond to surrounding changes by automatically switching air conditioners based on environmental measurements. For instance, cities achieve a remarkable reduction of costs in heating, ventilation, and air conditioning (HVAC) by placing Internet of Things (IoT)-powered cooling systems to optimize HVAC usage based on the activities in each room [26].

Moreover, the latest developments in power (and micro) grids allow the consumer to monitor electricity consumption in real time. The latter increases the reliability of power transmission, optimizes the required supply level, and minimizes the consumption cost. Evolving technology, empowered by advances in shallow and deep learning, analyzes patterns in city-wide energy consumption to only deliver an optimal amount. Additionally, cities use sensors to detect pipe leaks; New York city saved more than $73 million in water costs by notifying residents about possible (predicted) water leaks [26]. The latter becomes possible after the deployment of smart water meters and by exploiting advanced data analysis algorithms. Some smart solutions engage the citizens to contribute to the economic sustainability of the cities. They encourage people to adapt utility usage patterns both in volume and in timeframe.

These are only a few examples of the innovative approaches cities worldwide take to support the sustainability of the environment.

Smart Safety

As crime evolves and becomes more high-tech, public safety and security demand novel approaches from local governments to protect the citizens. Data-driven approaches play an increasingly important role in crime prevention. In fact, by using a system of connected video feeds, the city of Rio de Janeiro has improved the response time of emergency [11] and Chicago has reduced violent crime by using predictive crime heat maps to aid police efforts [17].

Smart Mobility

Data-driven transportation systems address the issues of congestion and pollution, manage parking and public transportation, advance road safety, and enhance shipment schedules. To this end, these solutions integrate data from various sources, such as geographically distributed traffic and weather sensors, cameras, and GPS, to apply algorithmic analyses while offering optimal paths. For instance, IoT devices collect data regarding road situations and routing the forthcoming travelers to eliminate congestion [21]. Furthermore, data exchange among vehicles through IoT and the Internet of Vehicles (IoV) supports traffic efficiency and safety [14].

Smart Economy

Smart economy solutions aim to strengthen the municipal economy and incorporate policies and procedures to encourage innovation for sustainability and motivate collaboration between citizens and private and public sectors [16]. These solutions manifest in many forms and applications that possess unique characteristics, challenges, and approaches. For instance, the local government of Dublin encourages a combination of data-driven techniques and networked infrastructure to foster economic growth and entrepreneurship. To this end, the open platform provides access to the city data, including real-time feeds. In addition, local leaders attract investments and support collaborative events for start-ups [28].

1.2.2.5   Management Tier

The strategic development of the smart city is a crucial component for the success of the respective projects [7]. The *management tier* addresses this essential task and also involves service provisioning, asset management, and security. City managers must balance technology, economic gains, and other public values to ensure the transformation into a smart city [3].

Both local authorities and individual organizations or service providers can lead transformational projects and play a central role in their implementation. Moreover, technology enthusiasts can also offer their vision of smart city initiatives.

1.2.2.6   Stakeholder Tier

A *stakeholder tier* in the reference architecture represents the individuals, teams, organizations, or groups interested in realizing transformational projects. In a smart city setting, these groups include but are not limited to:

- **Local governments** are interested in the effectiveness of the city services and natural resource consumption and the readiness of the municipalities to face the challenges of the growing population [18].
- **Citizens** expect the city services will meet their expectations effectively and efficiently. The participation of the residents in a decision-making process is vital to promote inclusion.
- **Software developers** and technology enthusiasts design and use smart city services and applications.

- **Service providers and operators** engage in the development of the efficient services and their maintenance, as well as providing support to the citizens.
- **Academic research** plays a crucial role in the development of the cities by developing new models and prototypes of the practical systems [12].

It is vital to consider each stakeholder group's needs and engage them in developing a sustainable and safe smart city to ensure the project's success. Political stability and transparency of the projects, effective policies and communication, effective project coordination, using the latest technologies, and human rights are among the core factors to consider ensuring the sufficient engagement level of the stakeholders in smart city projects [15].

1.3 Summary

To address the challenges in urbanization, worldwide municipal governments and private companies strategize transformative projects to solve the issues and improve the efficiency of the city operations. Luckily, technological progress offers a remarkable opportunity to employ technology, data, and advanced analytical strategies to improve the lives of millions of urban residents. However, planning and implementing such projects is a complex endeavor that relies on the technological development of the particular city and requires the engagement of many disciplines, including engineering, computer science, health, social science, and alike. Nevertheless, the successful transformational projects inspire growth and coalition of cities to solve common problems. The collaboration of citizens and private and public sectors positively affected the effectiveness and sustainability of city operational functions. The chapter elaborated on various challenges of modern municipalities and introduced the concept of a smart city.

References

1. Research and Markets.   Global smart cities market by focus area, smart transportation, smart buildings, smart utilities, smart citizen services (public safety, smart healthcare, smart education, smart street lighting, e-governance), and region - forecast to 2026. https://www.researchandmarkets.com/reports/5146372/global-smart-cities-market-by-focus-area-smart. Accessed: 2022-05-07.
2. Zubair A Baig, Patryk Szewczyk, Craig Valli, Priya Rabadia, Peter Hannay, Maxim Chernyshev, Mike Johnstone, Paresh Kerai, Ahmed Ibrahim, Krishnun Sansurooah, and others. Future challenges for smart cities: Cyber-security and digital forensics. *Digital Investigation*, 22:3–13, 2017.
3. Vita Santa Barletta, Danilo Caivano, Giovanni Dimauro, Antonella Nannavecchia, and Michele Scalera. Managing a smart city integrated model through smart program management. *Applied Sciences*, 10(2):714, 2020.

4. United States Census Burea. U.S. and world population clock. Accessed: 2022-05-07.
5. UN Chronicle. The evolution and challenges of security within cities. https://www.un.org/en/chronicle/article/evolution-and-challenges-security-within-cities, 2018. Accessed: 2022-05-07.
6. L. Cui, G. Xie, Y. Qu, L. Gao, and Y. Yang. Security and Privacy in Smart Cities: Challenges and Opportunities. *IEEE Access*, 6:46134–46145, 2018.
7. Mengbing Du, Xiaoling Zhang, and Luca Mora. Strategic planning for smart city development: assessing spatial inequalities in the basic service provision of metropolitan cities. *Journal of Urban Technology*, 28(1–2):115–134, 2021.
8. Ramzi El-Haddadeh, Vishanth Weerakkody, Mohamad Osmani, Dhaval Thakker, and Kawaljeet Kaur Kapoor. Examining citizens' perceived value of internet of things technologies in facilitating public sector services engagement. *Government Information Quarterly*, 36(2):310–320, 2019.
9. CRED EM-DAT. The international disaster database. *Center for Research on the Epidemiology of Disasters. Disponivel em. https://www.emdat.be*, 2022.
10. A. Gharaibeh, M. A. Salahuddin, S. J. Hussini, A. Khreishah, I. Khalil, M. Guizani, and A. Al-Fuqaha. Smart Cities: A Survey on Data Management, Security, and Enabling Technologies. *IEEE Communications Surveys Tutorials*, 19(4):2456–2501, 2017.
11. IBM. City of Rio de Janeiro and IBM Collaborate to Advance Emergency Response System; Access to Real-Time Information Empowers Citizens. https://www.prnewswire.com/news-releases/city-of-rio-de-janeiro-and-ibm-collaborate-to-advance-emergency-response-system-access-to-real-time-information-empowers-citizens-133545433.html. Accessed: 2020-04-09.
12. Inete Ielite, Gregory Olevsky, and Timurs Safiulins. Identification and prioritization of stakeholders in the planning process of sustainable development of the smart city. In *2015 IEEE Seventh International Conference on Intelligent Computing and Information Systems (ICICIS)*, pages 251–257. IEEE, 2015.
13. Sidra Ijaz, Munam Ali Shah, Abid Khan, and Mansoor Ahmed. Smart cities: A survey on security concerns. *International Journal of Advanced Computer Science and Applications*, 7(2):612–625, 2016.
14. Elvira Ismagilova, Laurie Hughes, Yogesh K Dwivedi, and K Ravi Raman. Smart cities: Advances in research—an information systems perspective. *International Journal of Information Management*, 47:88–100, 2019.
15. Nimesha Sahani Jayasena, KGAS Waidyasekara, Harshini Mallawaarachchi, and Sanduni Peiris. Ensuring engagement of stakeholders in smart city projects: case study in Sri Lanka. *Journal of Urban Planning and Development*, 147(4):05021045, 2021.
16. Vinod Kumar and Bharat Dahiya. Smart economy in smart cities. In *Smart economy in smart cities*, pages 3–76. Springer, 2017.
17. Timothy Mclaughlin. As shootings soar, Chicago police use technology to predict crime. https://www.reuters.com/article/us-chicago-police-technology/as-shootings-soar-chicago-police-use-technology-to-predict-crime-idUSKBN1AL08P. Accessed: 2020-04-09.
18. Taewoo Nam and Theresa A Pardo. Smart city as urban innovation: Focusing on management, policy, and context. In *Proceedings of the 5th international conference on theory and practice of electronic governance*, pages 185–194, 2011.
19. United Nations. 68% of the world population projected to live in urban areas by 2050. https://www.un.org/development/desa/en/news/population/2018-revision-of-world-urbanization-prospects.html. Accessed: 2020-04-15.
20. OECD. The OECD programme on smart cities and inclusive growth. Accessed: 2022-05-07.
21. Bhagya Nathali Silva, Murad Khan, and Kijun Han. Towards sustainable smart cities: A review of trends, architectures, components, and open challenges in smart cities. *Sustainable Cities and Society*, 38:697–713, 2018.
22. SmartCitiesWorld. City profile. https://www.smartcitiesworld.net/smart-cities-profile. Accessed: 2020-04-25.

23. M. Sookhak, H. Tang, Y. He, and F. R. Yu. Security and Privacy of Smart Cities: A Survey, Research Issues and Challenges. *IEEE Communications Surveys Tutorials*, 21(2):1718–1743, 2019.
24. Jun Sun and Marshall Scott Poole. Beyond connection: situated wireless communities. *Communications of the ACM*, 53(6):121–125, 2010.
25. Ling Min Tan, Hadi Arbabi, Danielle Densley Tingley, Paul E Brockway, and Martin Mayfield. Mapping resource effectiveness across urban systems. *npj Urban Sustainability*, 1(1):1–14, 2021.
26. Ashley Theron-Ord. Singapore uses IoT to create smart building. https://www.smart-energy.com/regional-news/asia/singapore-iot-smart-buildings/. Accessed: 2020-04-15.
27. Patrick Henry Winston. *Artificial intelligence*. Addison-Wesley Longman Publishing Co., Inc., 1992.
28. Smart Cities World. Dublin.

Chapter 2
Cyber Brittleness of Smart Cities

Given the extensive worldwide growth of smart cities, it is intuitive and essential to acknowledge the debilitating and disrupting effects of cyber-attacks on these initiatives. With the embedding of the latest technologies varying from telecommunication enablers to advances in data-driven artificial intelligence (AI), smart cities and their critical infrastructure are now accessible through network communications. However, the adversaries can use the network-connected infrastructure to put the human population in danger, if, for instance, they gain remote control over the automated operations to compromise services.

Protecting smart cities from cyber-attacks is a crucial mission for their survival. Although cybersecurity is among the critical challenges for smart cities, examining cyber threats is tricky due to the complexity of a smart city's architecture, its contradictory security requirements, and its use of extensive (vulnerable) software. Nevertheless, numerous real-world attacks impair the trustworthiness of smart cities, thus hindering the achievement of their full potential. Therefore, it is imperative to consider and explore the cyber threat landscape of smart cities.

In Sect. 2.1, this chapter identifies the fundamental peculiarities of smart city cybersecurity. In Sect. 2.2, it raises awareness regarding past real-world cyber incidents that affected smart cities. Furthermore, in Sect. 2.3, this chapter examines prevailing threats targeting smart cities that are identified from actual and potential cyber-attacks. Section 2.4 concludes the chapter.

2.1 Cybersecurity of Smart Cities vs Enterprise IT Security

Cybersecurity concerns in a smart city environment have become an active topic from research and operational perspectives. Although there are many similarities with enterprise IT security, several fundamental peculiarities of smart cities prevent the full realization of the traditional standards and methodologies for cybersecurity.

N. Neshenko et al., *Smart Cities: Cyber Situational Awareness to Support Decision Making*, https://doi.org/10.1007/978-3-031-18464-2_2

One significant attribute of network-connected critical infrastructure is the requirement of the continuous availability of Industrial Control Systems (ICSs) that provide partial or complete autonomation of the decision-making process. These real-time availability constraints are usually more rigid than most traditional IT systems, where confidentiality usually plays the first role.

In addition, the complexity of the interaction between many infrastructure components exponentially increases the impact of cyber-attacks. In addition, the central authority that manages all these components might not even exist. Furthermore, legacy anomaly detection cannot keep up with rapid agility, and data-greedy methods that employ malicious signatures to detect attacks continue to lack behind.

The most significant difference between smart city infrastructure and other IT systems is their close coupling with the physical world. Traditional methods and techniques of computer and information security are focused on requirements such as confidentiality, integrity, and availability. However, smart cities bring new frontiers to the attacks, so significant consideration should be given to the investigation of the attack impact on the estimation and control algorithms, as well as on the impact on the physical world and the well-being of citizens.

There are several additional concerns that make smart city cybersecurity unique: heterogeneity and geographical distribution of the infrastructure, often the limited computational capabilities of connected devices, legacy equipment, difficulties with security and privacy measurements, and inconsistencies within security requirements for different systems.

2.2   Cyber Incidents: Decades in Retrospect

The exponential deployment and reliance on connected technical systems opened new opportunities for cybercriminals aiming to leverage vulnerable infrastructure. Cities around the world continue to fall the victims of cyber-attackers, who aim to the extent the impact of their actions by using numerous tactics, resulting in countless harmful outcomes. The latter includes but is not limited to physical damage to the expensive equipment, loss of access to and control over critical services and resources such as water and energy supply, and alike. Unsurprisingly, cybersecurity has become a critical matter for smart cities [32].

Attackers often hind behind clouds and use advanced machine learning algorithms to exploit evolving technologies to amplify the attack's possibilities [23] and thus the impact. The effect is evident in an attack on a power grid that left nearly 225,000 residents of three Ukrainian regions without electric power [7]. Another city, Baltimore, lost irreplaceable law enforcement-related data and fell a target of a ransomware attack on its emergency service. This attack led to the disruption of the emergency assistance operation [18]. The lack of cyber-resilient IoT devices allowed hackers to cause malfunctioning road signs [33] and cause distress in Dallas by turning on the hurricane sirens in the middle of the night [3].

The attackers also target network-connected water facilities raising concerns about the water contamination problem [46, 49].

The past decade witnessed a distinct shift in cyber threat incidents, with ransomware becoming the most substantial cybersecurity threat faced by smart cities, irrespective of their location or abused sector [43]. Recent global cyber incidents include attacks against power distribution systems, water and wastewater systems, government facilities, health care providers, and transportation systems [21]. To increase awareness and facilitate joint efforts for the prevention of cyber-attacks, the U.S. Congress recently passed the Cyber Incident Reporting for Critical Infrastructure Act of 2022 (CIRCIA) [30]. It requires critical infrastructure organizations, which include financial, energy companies, and other key businesses for which a disruption would impact economic security or public health and safety, to report substantial cybersecurity incidents or ransom payments to the federal government.

Despite the growing concerns and investments in cybersecurity, the cyber threats targeting smart cities are rapidly expanding; the tendency of sophisticated and widespread cyber-attacks contains the targets such as local governance and private industry [37]. We now provide an overview of several reported cyber incidents (Fig. 2.1), as discussed in the open-source literature. The list of attacks is by no means comprehensive but rather a riffle through the important incidents to illustrate the variety and impact of the cyber incidents on the infrastructure that supports smart cities. Several of presented incidents are discussed in this section in reverse chronological order.

2.2.1 The Colonial Pipeline Attack

Background Colonial Pipeline Company provides pipeline services to deliver gasoline, kerosene, home heating oil, diesel, national defense fuels, and refined petroleum products across the United States. Daily company's throughput constitutes roughly 2.5 million barrels of fuel transported from the Gulf Coast to the Eastern Seaboard.

Incident In April 2021, malicious actors gained access to the network of Colonial Pipeline Company using a virtual private network account that allows the employees to access the company computer network remotely [12]. Although the user account was not active at the attack, it still retained privileges to access the network. Later, in May, the employee received a ransom note demanding cryptocurrency. The entire pipeline was shut down immediately following the response procedure to prevent severe damage. The five-day outage led to a fuel supply shortage, resulting in lengthy lines at gas stations and higher fuel prices.

Lessons Learned A single compromised password became a cause of the shortages across the East Coast. This incident highlights the importance of rigorous

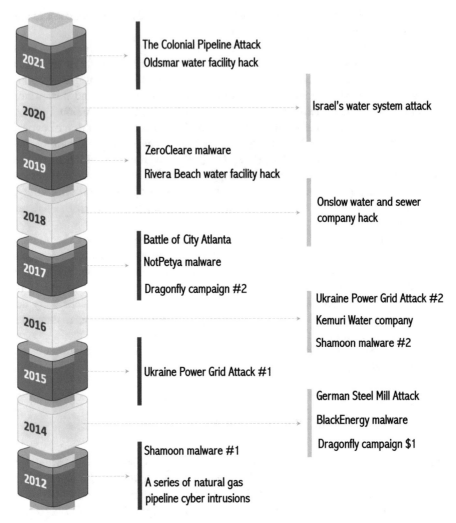

Fig. 2.1 Timeline of cyber-attacks targeting smart cities during 2012–2021 (not exhaustive)

procedures for access control and revoking access privileges when the user account is no more in use.

2.2.2   Israel's Water System Attack

Incident In 2020, an attacker terrorized Israel's water system by conducting two cyber-attacks. One of the attacks targeted agricultural water pumps in the upper Galilee. Another one hit infrastructure in the center of the country and aimed at increasing chlorine levels in water flowing to residential areas. The water authority confirmed the incidents, assuring that no damage was done to Israel's water system [50].

Lessons Learned The incident confirmed one more time that the landscape of the targets of cyber-attacks in water systems is wide and may include water treatment and irrigation systems.

2.2.3 Onslow Water and Sewer Company Hack

Background Onslow Water and Sewer Authority, a water utility company in Jacksonville (North Carolina) [56] that serves about 54,744 water and 7221 sewer accounts.

Incident In October 2018, Onslow Water and Sewer Company fell victim to a ransomware attack [47]. The attack began by spreading a virus known as EMOTET; the virus was detected by the company team and passed for investigation by security experts outside the company. However, an attacker did not lose valuable time and launched a more sophisticated virus known as RYUK. Although the response team immediately disconnected the facility from the Internet, the virus reached its goal and encrypted data. Following encryption, the authorities received an email demanding payment to unlock data. Criminals did not receive payment since the company refused to negotiate.

Lessons Learned Ransomware is a fast-growing threat, targeting users of all types, and smart cities are not excluded. A proper mechanism should be introduced to protect critical infrastructure from this threat. Since then, the joint advisory body of the Federal Bureau of Investigation (FBI), the Cybersecurity and Infrastructure Agency (CISA), the Environmental Protection Agency (EPA), and the National Security Agency (NSA) have issued around 30 mitigation tactics to prevent, detect, and respond to cyber threats and urged water and wastewater facilities use risk analysis to determine more suitable ones for the system [8]. In response to the inevitable threat, the U.S. administration plans to increase resources available for public water systems to boost their cybersecurity [31].

2.2.4 Battle of City Atlanta

Background Atlanta is a city and capital of the U.S. state of Georgia. The population of this popular city is about 500,000 residents.

Incident In March 2018, critical systems operated in the city of Atlanta experienced massive outages as ransomware named SamSam spread through the network [24]. The municipality response team immediately shut out employees' computers from their systems. The response team put offline numerous city services, such as online bill paying, as a precautious. Given that a court system was incapacitated, police were forced to file paper reports until the services were brought back online.

Later, this notable hack was classified as the largest successful breach of security for a major American city by ransomware; it impacted about 6 million city residents. The city authorities refused to pay the demand of the attacker of $51,000 to restore Atlanta's systems to full functionality. However, the price Atlanta city paid to restore lost data is estimated to be over $2.6 million, with the additional $9.5 million requested later [45].

Lessons Learned The incident stressed the importance of data management policies that include regular backup. It also highlights the need for a least access privilege policy and regularity in patching critical systems.

2.2.5   Kemuri Water Company

Background An undisclosed water utility in the USA, shown under the pseudonym of Kemuri Water Company.

Incident In 2016, an attacker gained access to a control application responsible for manipulating hundreds of PLCs of the undisclosed water treatment plant [54]. Furthermore, an attacker altered the number of induced chemicals and affected water treatment and production capabilities. According to Verizon, a Syria hacktivist group was behind the attack. The Kemuri attack can have a catastrophic effect on the community. Subsequently, a comprehensive assessment was conducted on both operational technologies and information systems. It revealed numerous vulnerabilities with a high-risk level, including one that is related to the reliance on outdated computers and operating systems.

Lessons Learned The incident pinpointed the necessity of several strategies that can protect ICS deployed in critical infrastructure from cyber-attacks. Among others, having Internet-facing ICSs is a flawed practice for critical infrastructure due to the consequences on society.

2.2.6   Ukraine Power Grid Attack

Background Prykarpattyaoblenergo JSC is an electricity distribution and sales company serving the Ivano-Frankivsk region—the western region of Ukraine.

Incident   In December 2015, the power company Prykarpattyaoblenergo located in western Ukraine suffered a power outage [41]. Cyber attackers rendered SCADA equipment inoperable. The investigation found that BlackEnergy malware, which was planted using spear-phishing, exploited macros in Microsoft Excel documents. This first successful cyber-attack on a power grid cut electricity to nearly a quarter-million Ukrainians and kept them in the dark for about six hours. The incident happened during the ongoing Russian military invasion in Ukraine, and it was connected to the malicious activity performed by Russia's civilian and military intelligence services.

Lessons Learned   The attack demonstrated the possibility of damaging the power grid through cyber means. Although the attacker used relatively unsophisticated techniques, the impact was significant. The incident stressed the importance of education regarding phishing attacks and continuous system patching.

2.2.7   German Steel Mill Attack

Background   In its 2014 annual report, the German Federal Office for Information Security noted that a malicious actor had infiltrated a steel facility [6]. The report, however, did not provide the name of the facility.

Incident   The attackers used spear-phishing and social engineering tactics to gain access to the corporate network of the steel plant and then managed penetration into the production network. The attack caused multiple failures of ICS assets, eventually deterring a blast furnace from shutting down in a controlled manner, causing "massive damage to the plant" [6]. The description of the incident in the report led many to consider the intentional damage to the plant.

Lessons Learned   The significant lesson learned from the incident is the demonstration of the capabilities of the malicious actors using traditional, well-known attack techniques such as APT with the intention to impact an operation of the critical assets.

2.2.8   The Cyber-Attack on Saudi Aramco

Background   Saudi Aramco (Saudi Arabian Oil Company) is the state-owned company accountable for the exploration, production, and refining of oil reserves. At the time of the cyber-attack discussed below, the market value of the company was estimated to be around $10 trillion USD, making it the world's most valuable company [20]. Given that the threats against Aramco can have a harmful effect on the national security of Saudi Arabia, the Kingdom heavily invested in securing Aramco facilities and provided constant armed force [9] to secure perimeter.

Incident In August 2012, a Saudi Aramco oil company fell victim to a cyber-attack that wiped off 30,000 computers and forced the company to keep several internal networks disabled for a period of several weeks [40]. The attack that was conducted by using a malware labeled Shamoon was considered as an attack not only against a single company but rather as an attack against the economy [1].

Lessons Learned The attack became a wake-up call to seriously consider the cyber resilience of the global energy supply.

2.3 Adversary Model

The actual cyber incidents indicate the successful or semi-successful attacks to exploit a wide variety of vulnerabilities and cause direct or indirect disruption of services delivered by smart cities. Although cyber threat landscape depends on the development progress and the underlying architecture of a particular smart city, to generalize, this section examines prevalent threats targeting smart cities that are identified from actual and potential cyber-attacks. Smart cities are vulnerable to traditional computer viruses, eavesdropping, software hijacking, memory exploits, hardware failure, human errors, and electrical interruption. However, these threats are excluded from this study. The connection with the physical environment, the introduction of IoT devices, and the emergence of new communication protocols, as well as employing machine learning algorithms, induce new security threats and amplify the impact of traditional exposures [36].

2.3.1 Attackers

The discussed cyber events provide important insights into the capabilities of key threat actors and their persistence in causing physical damage. This section describes several potential attackers and their motivations and resources.

Insider: disgruntled employees who understand ICS assets functions and processes are one of the dangerous origins of targeted cyber-attacks against smart cities. These malicious actors not only have authorized access to computers and networks that connect ICS assets but also possess insider knowledge that can signify the attack impact. One of the unprecedented incidents is an attack on Maroochy Shire Council's sewage system in Queensland, Australia [49]. The offender was a former employee who failed to secure his job. He managed to keep his attack stealthy and released about 1 million liters of untreated sewage into a stormwater drain jeopardizing the well-being of citizens. Another incident happened in Sacramento, California, USA [26], where a computer technician was trying to shut down the power grid. Luckily, no blackout occurred because, however, it costs $14,000 to repair the damage.

Outsider cybercriminals are the malicious actors that compromise cyberspace anytime anywhere. Although the attacks can random, they may cause dramatic effect on smart city operations. For instance, malware planted in the network that connects traditional IT and ICS can render inappropriate control response of the latter, as happened in 2003 of power plant in Ohio [42].

Organized cyber criminals is a well-organized network of hackers, programmers, and other technically savvy specialists who combine their skills to execute immense and potentially devastating attacks. Here are the five notorious cyber groups that terrorize the Internet and smart cities, in particular.

COVELLITE targets networks of civilian electric energy worldwide and gathers intelligence on intellectual property and internal industrial operations [11].

LAZARUS GROUP is allegedly a North Korean group that is believed to be a group behind the 2017 WannaCry Ransomware that paralyzed the health system operations for several days and caused havoc and social distress [16].

DRAGONFLY is a Cyber Espionage group that is well known for targeting cyber supply chain (CSC) organizations [35].

KAMACITE group has targeted mostly electric utilities, oil and gas operations, and various manufacturing [22].

SANDWORM is allegedly a Russian cyber military cyber intelligence unit. This group is believed to be behind the 2015 and 2016 Ukraine power cyber incidents [19] and represent the next category of the attackers.

State-sponsored attackers may cause a more significant threat to smart city infrastructure than individual adversaries. One of the publicly known cyber-attacks against the Ukrainian power grid that left in the dark about 250,000 people is connected to the malicious activity performed by Russia's civilian and military intelligence services [41] during the ongoing military Russian military invasion into Ukraine. Cyber-attacks against critical infrastructure that is a significant component of smart cities can become a new military power in international conflicts.

2.3.2 Impact of Cyber-Attacks

The main goals of malicious actions against smart cities are to manipulate the integrity and availability of electronic devices, services, data, privacy, and confidentiality violation and to damage the infrastructural environment. The broader impact of such attacks on critical infrastructure, which is deployed in smart cities, lies in the safety of the ecosystem and may affect public health. With this said, the impact

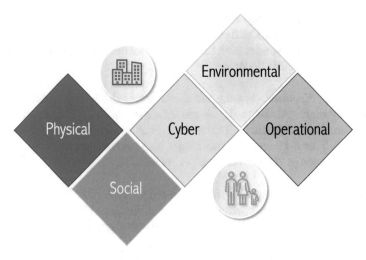

Fig. 2.2 Categories of the impact of cyber-attacks against smart cities

of the attack encompasses the effect on the physical, cyber, operational, social, and environmental frontiers of smart cities (Fig. 2.2) and results in immediate disruption or long-term damage or loss.

Physical Impact

Attacks aiming to cause damage, breakdown, or destroy engineered equipment and property result in a *physical impact*. Malicious actors may cause short-term damage in the form of system performance reduction. For instance, a system can temporarily slow down (or completely shut down) provided service. As it was with Colonial Pipeline, ransomware caused major disruption of the pipeline so that it could not maintain the daily required amount of fuel to the East Coast [12].

The adversary can also provoke long-term physical damage or entire destruction of the attacked system that supports the goals of smart cities. Depending on the severity of the property damage, it may extend the impact to public and environmental safety concerns. This hazard went beyond theoretical when in 2000, police arrested a man who used a radio transmitter to take control over the Maroochy wastewater system and released one million liters of untreated sewage directly into the waterway [49].

Cyber Impact

Various cyber-attacks directly target digital data, threatening confidentiality, integrity, and availability. An attacker operates numerous tactics to support their goal. Of such tactics is spreading malware that gains access to sensitive data and applying the cryptographical algorithm to make it inaccessible and unreadable for legitimate users. For example, the malware SamSam held hostage the services provided by numerous cities. This example shows how data tampering can sabotage data-dependent functions and results in massive data loss [24].

Operational Impact
The effect of attacks aiming to disrupt services and manipulate the availability and integrity of connected components of smart cities is classified as *operational impact*. The impact can be visible immediately in the form of loss of control, visibility, productivity, and service availability or may have long-term effects such as legal liability and operational information loss. An adversary can use various techniques to evade detection and cause long-lingering harm.

In some scenarios, the impact of the loss of control can be extended to environmental damage or social distress, as happened with the hack of the Ukrainian power grid that left nearly a quarter of a million people in the dark for a long period of time [41].

Social Impact
Metropolitan residents are the primary users of urban infrastructure and smart solutions. Therefore, it is vital to acknowledge the impact of a cyber-attack in smart city realms on society. The attacker, for instance, can gain access to the private information shared by the citizens with local authorities, thus violating residents' privacy or aiming at identity theft. Furthermore, the cyber-attack can cause social distress, similar to the incident in Dallas when the attacker gained access to a hurricane siren and raised a false alarm in the middle of the night [3]. In more extreme cases, the attacker can threaten the safety of the residents, as happened in Poland when an attacker gained control over a smart tram and caused injuries. These and other incidents hinder the implementation of smart city initiatives and may cost a reputation and political repercussions to city leaders.

Environmental Impact
Cyber-attacks on smart cities can cause an environmental catastrophe. Therefore, cybersecurity professionals and city leaders should carefully address the cybersecurity of critical infrastructure with more significant attention.

In summary, Fig. 2.3 outlines the impact of cyber-attacks and their corresponding categories.

2.3.3 Categorization of Cyber Threats

The cyber events discussed in this chapter increase visibility into techniques used in cyber-attacks. The classification of cyber threats varies; we consider four following classes of threats—exploratory threats, infrastructure threats, data threats, and third-party vulnerabilities—depicted in Fig. 2.4.

First, the class *"discovery threat"* consists of the threats aiming to enumerate resources and credentials. Second, *"infrastructure threats"* represents threats aiming to destroy or gain control of smart city infrastructure by deploying malware and reprogramming or overwhelming core resources. Third, the class *"data threats"* consists of threats which endeavor to undermine data confidentiality and integrity,

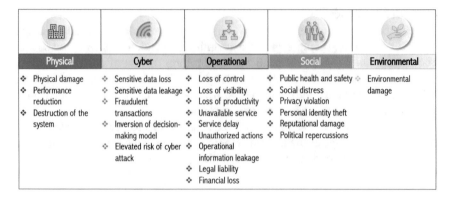

Fig. 2.3 Impact of cyber-attacks by category

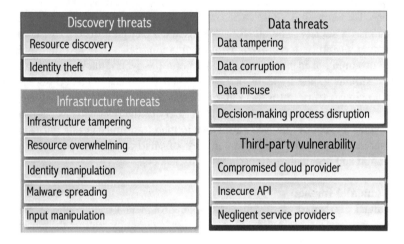

Fig. 2.4 Threat landscape of smart cities

as well as destabilize machine learning algorithms. Finally, *"third-party vulnerabilities"* refers to threats targeting service providers which produce a profound effect on smart cities' activities and security.

2.3.3.1 Discovery Threats

The first step of any attack is the exploratory step, during which an attacker gathers valuable intelligence about the target. It starts by infiltrating target assets (e.g., exposed systems, devices) in order to explore possible points of entry of the system.

Network connection enumeration. To index vulnerable assets that have been deployed in smart cities, the attacker can perform several actions.

- By conducting **an active Internet-scale probing** [15]. Besides being the first step of any cyber-attack, active probing significantly impairs network performance leading to delaying response time of users' requests [38]. The adversary can use tools such as netstat [55] or similar tools to gather information about the connected node.
- By using the **search engine for Internet-connected devices** like Shodan [14], which crawls the Internet 24/7 and updates its repository in real time to provide a recent list of IoT devices. By grabbing and analyzing banners and device metadata, Shodan conducts testing for various vulnerabilities including Heartbleed, Logjam, and default passwords. Alternatively, the search engine Censys [13] collects data (including IoT information) through executing horizontal scans of the public IPv4 address space and provides public access to raw data through a web service. These and other engines, while being a valuable source for cybersecurity research and operation, allow to discover easy targets, identify open ports, indexing responsive devices' header or banner information [39]. Collected data can include device type, its vendor and model, firmware version, and other sensitive information that can be used to further exploit the respective device and gain access to the network.
- By **eavesdropping**, which is an unpermitted listening to communication to capture the network communication patterns and obtain the network map. It can result in a violation of confidentiality and integrity.

Cyber identity theft involves obtaining the user identity, which can then be exploited to gain privileged access to the system or data. The threat comes in different forms:

- After an attacker compromises a computer, **extracting user credentials from hashes** is a relatively straightforward task that can be performed using various available tools and techniques.
- An attacker can use a broad range of malicious activities, collectively known as **social engineering**, to conduct a cyber-attack through human interaction. An attacker can use personal information or manipulative actions to prompt users to make security mistakes and give away sensitive personal cyber details such as user credentials, passwords, etc.
- Aiming at stealing sensitive digital data like credit card and login credentials or installing malware on the victim's machine, an attacker performs **phishing** attacks. These attacks can arrive in fraudulent communication via email asking a victim to provide sensitive data.
- By **leveraging weak or default credentials** of IoT devices. An attacker may leverage the default credentials of IoT devices or control systems. These default credentials are provided by manufacturers for the initial installation of the device and are usually well documented and may be available online. While modifying default credentials is a necessary strategy, a myriad of Internet-connected devices with hard-coded or default credentials remain in use rendering it possible for an attacker to search or brute-force the default credentials to leverage them for an

Discovery Threats	Impact				
	Physical	Cyber	Operational	Social	Environmental
Resource discovery Respective attacks: ➢ Active probing ➢ Discovery through search engine	❖ Performance reduction	❖ Elevated risk of cyber attack	❖ Unavailable service ❖ Service delay		
Identity theft Respective attacks: ➢ Social engineering ➢ Phishing ➢ Search for default credentials		❖ Elevated risk of cyber attack	❖ Operational information leakage	❖ Privacy violation ❖ Personal identity theft ❖ Political repercussions	

Fig. 2.5 Discovery threats in smart cities' settings: attacks and impacts

attack [10]. Given that many smart cities rely on IoT sensors, using weak or default credentials can lead to dramatic events.

Additionally, the costs of credentials theft come in the form of unauthorized access to smart cities' resources.

Furthermore, as summarized in Fig. 2.5, an adversary would almost always employ various methods to enumerate the deployed infrastructure.

2.3.3.2 Infrastructure Threats

One of the attacker's motivation is to gain illegitimate control over the infrastructure through tampering, manipulating, reprogramming, or overwhelming the resources.

Infrastructure tampering. This threat could be manifested in the following ways:

- By **direct physical access**. Given that a large number of actuators and sensors operate in an unattended manner with limited tamper-resistance methodologies and policies, a malicious actor can take advantage of physical proximity to a device. An attacker can cause intentional significant damage, alter the device services, or gain an unlimited access to data stored on its memory. In fact, compromised actuators that control the physical infrastructure (e.g., heating, switching elements, etc.) can provoke damage to physical objects and threaten public safety.
- By **botnet recruitment**, causing both direct and indirect adverse effects. The direct impact comes in the form of lost control over the infrastructure rendering the critical functions of a smart city at risk. Furthermore, the bots are often used by the attacker to launch Distributed Denial of Service (DDoS) attacks, collecting information from the network [48], mine cryptocurrency [58], spread malware [5], or conduct any other malicious activities. The indirect impact can cause system performance degradation, in addition to legal and compliance liability.
- By **exploiting firmware vulnerabilities**. Maliciously altered firmware induces a functional disruption of the targeted device [4]. By performing reverse engineering, the attacker can learn the functionality of the firmware update mechanism

and subsequently modify the configuration file to inject malicious code into a firmware update. The limitation of Programmable Logic Controllers (PLCs), however, hinders the implementation of a robust algorithm that would attempt to verify data integrity [2].

Resources overwhelming. The adversaries here seek to prevent access to the service and cause its disruption. To this end, the attacker can use different techniques, both straightforward and sophisticated.

- An attacker can **flood the target with excessive requests**, preventing the service from processing all requests in a timely manner and, therefore, legitimate users cannot gain access. This threat is even bigger for IoT-based smart cities since IoT is known to have limited computational capabilities. As an example, a smart building management system in one of the apartment buildings in Finland was flooded with bogus requests forcing heating devices to go offline [25].
- An attacker can **drain energy from the smart cities' infrastructure**. Due to strict safety regulations and radio propagation limitations, embedded devices are prevented from efficient energy harvesting [51]. Besides, poor software development practices often significantly increase energy consumption [17] leading to delays in operation.

Identity manipulation. This threat could originate into two different ways:

- By **introducing fake node** into the network to manipulate the identity of compromised devices aiming to maliciously influence the network. The introduction of malicious nodes often leads to the degradation of an overall network performance [44].
- By **using unauthorized API keys**.
- By **masquerading**, an attacker attempts to gain illegitimate access to information by impersonating a legitimate network node jeopardizing the network integrity and data manipulation or corruption.

Malware infection. An attacker spreads malware with the intent to infect smart sensors, IoT devices, or data servers. To this end, adversary attempts to change their functions or leak sensitive data. For instance, sending fake overload status from a wide range of smart meters could force several segments of the grid services to become offline.

Figure 2.6 illustrates attacks associated with this category and their impact on smart cities' operations.

2.3.3.3 Data Threats

Data manipulation threats manifest in four different ways: data tampering, data corruption, data misuse, and decision-making process disruption.

Data tampering. Recently, widespread ransomware attacks paralyzed numerous smart cities.

Infrastructure Threats	Impact				
	Physical	Cyber	Operational	Social	Environmental
Infrastructure tampering Respective attacks: ➢ Direct physical access ➢ Botnet recruitment ➢ Exploiting firmware vulnerabilities	❖ Physical damage ❖ Destruction of the system	❖ Sensitive data loss ❖ Sensitive data leakage	❖ Operational information leakage ❖ Legal liability ❖ Financial loss	❖ Public health and safety	❖ Environmental damage
Resource overwhelming Respective attacks: ➢ Flood the target with excessive requests ➢ Drain energy from infrastructure	❖ Physical damage ❖ Performance reduction	❖ Elevated risk of cyber attack	❖ Loss of productivity ❖ Unavailable service ❖ Financial loss	❖ Public health and safety ❖ Social distress	❖ Environmental damage
Identity manipulation Respective attacks: ➢ Introducing fake node ➢ Using unauthorized API keys	❖ Performance reduction	❖ Elevated risk of cyber attack	❖ Loss of productivity ❖ Financial loss		❖ Environmental damage
Malware infection Respective attacks: ➢ Malware infection	❖ Physical damage ❖ Performance reduction ❖ Destruction of the system	❖ Sensitive data loss ❖ Sensitive data leakage ❖ Elevated risk of cyber attack	❖ Loss of control ❖ Loss of visibility ❖ Loss of productivity ❖ Operational information leakage ❖ Financial loss	❖ Public health and safety	❖ Environmental damage

Fig. 2.6 Infrastructure threats in smart cities' settings: attacks and impacts

- **Ransomware** is malicious software that locks hardware or encrypts data files until a monetary ransom is paid typically through cryptocurrencies. Due to the highly connected nature of smart cities, this type of threat has a massive impact on city operations. Additionally, if an adversary attacks vital sectors such as healthcare [34], the inability to access patient data could cost human lives. Moreover, we can quantify data tampering attacks in smart cities by measuring their financial loss. For instance, paid ransom, price of data recovery, and operation loss (e.g., free bus rides [18]) are several examples which assess the financial loss caused by such attacks.

Data corruption. The sabotage of the sensor data is quite dangerous in smart city environment.

- An attacker can use **false data injection** attack to fuse legitimate or corrupted input toward Internet-connected sensors to cause various integrity violations. Even though injecting malicious data into smart sensors might seem minimal [29], it could cause a dramatic economic effect, social distress, or jeopardize the safety and well-being of city residents [27]. For instance, smart meters can be used to steal energy from municipalities [57], or false emergency alerts can create created havoc, as happened in Dallas [33]. Furthermore, these malicious inputs can be crafted in such a way that they force machine learning models to make false predictions and cause instability in the city's operations.

Data misuse. Smart cities' infrastructure generates vast amounts of information. Indeed, this information is collected from a myriad of sensors and from citizens (when applicable, with their permission). Additionally, the information collected can be used to take advantage of personal information for various reasons.

- Aiming to **track the activity of the citizens through sensors or surveillance cameras**, an adversary can sniff the communication or leverage weak web access to steal personal credentials, which could, later on, be used for fraudulent transactions.
- The collected **data is used for unpermitted purposes** [53].

Disruption of decision-making process. The majority of smart cities implement machine learning algorithms as a decision engine; the cybersecurity decision-makers should consider the reliability of such algorithms. Attackers can disrupt the decision-making process by data poisoning or by instantiating an exploratory attack.

- The decision engine can be compromised by injecting adversarial samples into the training dataset. This malicious strategy is known as **data poisoning** and aims to compromise the learning process. The complexity of machine learning algorithms increases the difficulty in recognizing the correctness of the produced output rendering the significance of the vulnerability. Additionally, the trustworthiness of smart cities' analytics will continue to suffer until the robustness of such algorithms can be confirmed. This issue is equally relevant to the trustworthiness of intrusion detection systems backed by machine learning algorithms [52].
- In the **data exploratory strategy**, the adversary attempts to gather data by probing the learning algorithm (learner). An adversary, aiming at the model inversion of information inference, injects data samples that are designed to bypass the learner during the testing phase.

Figure 2.7 illustrates the attacks associated with this category and their impacts on smart cities' operations.

Data Threats	Impact				
	Physical	Cyber	Operational	Social	Environmental
Data tampering Respective attacks: ➢ Ransomware attack		❖ Sensitive data loss	❖ Loss of control ❖ Loss of visibility ❖ Unavailable service ❖ Legal liability ❖ Financial loss	❖ Public health and safety ❖ Social distress	❖ Environmental damage
Data corruption Respective attacks: ➢ False data injection	❖ Physical damage ❖ Performance reduction ❖ Destruction of the system	❖ Sensitive data loss ❖ Fraudulent transactions	❖ Loss of control ❖ Loss of productivity ❖ Unavailable service ❖ Service delay ❖ Legal liability ❖ Financial loss	❖ Public health and safety ❖ Social distress ❖ Reputational damage	❖ Environmental damage
Data misuse Respective attacks: ➢ Individual activity monitoring ➢ Unpermitted usage		❖ Sensitive data leakage ❖ Fraudulent transactions	❖ Financial loss	❖ Privacy violation ❖ Personal identity theft ❖ Reputational damage	
Disruption of decision-making process Respective attacks: ➢ Data poisoning ➢ Data exploratory attack	❖ Physical damage ❖ Performance reduction ❖ Destruction of the system	❖ Inversion of decision-making model ❖ Elevated risk of cyber attack	❖ Operational information leakage ❖ Financial loss	❖ Public health and safety ❖ Reputational damage	❖ Environmental damage

Fig. 2.7 Data threats in smart cities' settings: attacks and impacts

2.3.3.4 Third-Party Vulnerability

To augment the limitation of government budget and professional skills while promoting innovations and economic development, the administration of a smart city typically collaborates with the private sector. Private companies design and provide enabling technology, develop infrastructure, gather and process data, and produce software supporting decision-making. This strategic collaboration, however, brings cyber threats to a new edge.

Compromised cloud provider. Cloud computing brings a new frontier for the developers by proposing an infrastructure, platforms, and software over the Internet. Indeed, cloud services are an attractive option for ever-growing smart cities because of the low level of initial investments, their scalability, and continuous availability. However, the features of cloud computing, such as multi-tenancy and virtualization, can lead to the leakage of private information and unauthorized access. Representative examples of such attacks include those which

- Hijack cloud accounts
- Exploit system vulnerabilities [48].

Insecure API (Application Programming Interface) is a vulnerability that opens the doors to cloud applications and web services. API allows the users to customize their experience and receive access to many web services, including authentication and access control. Therefore, the impact of **API hijacking** depends on the service and shared information. For instance, in the city of Los Angeles, a clear text API key allowed a hacker to use paid Google services [28].

Negligent service provider. Some vendors introduce new cyber vulnerabilities. They can **intentionally or unintentionally leave backdoors** that allow attackers to access devices or software. They can further deploy IoT devices without patching capabilities. Although smart cities often operate unpatched, vulnerable products, some vendors are resistant to acknowledge security holes in their products, which endanger smart city service operators and subsequently the citizens.

Figure 2.8 illustrates such threats/vulnerabilities, associated attacks, and the impact of these attacks on smart cities.

2.4 Summary

Nowadays, cyberattacks have become an integral part of the day-by-day operation of cities worldwide. Financial loss, reputational damage, operational disruption, and legal liabilities are only a few examples of the potential impact of a cyber misdemeanor. But what raises the most concern is the catastrophic impact caused by cyber-attacks on critical infrastructure, which is a vital part of smart cities. Ransomware, command over control systems, and similar malicious incidents go further and affect millions of citizens: the massive hazard of cyber threats is rooted in the high coupling between different components of smart cities. The result

Third-party Vulnerability	Impact				
	Physical	Cyber	Operational	Social	Environmental
Compromised cloud provider Respective attacks ➢ Hijack cloud account ➢ Exploit system vulnerabilities		❖ Sensitive data loss ❖ Sensitive data leakage ❖ Elevated risk of cyberattack	❖ Loss of productivity ❖ Operational information leakage ❖ Financial loss	❖ Reputational damage	
Insecure API Respective attacks ➢ API hijacking		❖ Sensitive data leakage ❖ Elevated risk of cyberattack	❖ Loss of productivity ❖ Operational information leakage ❖ Financial loss	❖ Reputational damage	
Negligent service provider Respective attacks ➢ Intentional ➢ Unintentional		❖ Sensitive data leakage ❖ Elevated risk of cyberattack	❖ Loss of productivity ❖ Operational information leakage ❖ Financial loss	❖ Reputational damage	

Fig. 2.8 Third-party vulnerabilities threats in smart cities' settings: attacks and impacts

of the outage of essential services impacts the well-being and safety of citizens, jeopardizing national security.

The critical infrastructure sector widely uses intelligent technologies to provide valuable services to consumers; therefore, it is vulnerable to cybersecurity attacks. The look at recent cyber incidents targeting smart city infrastructure demonstrates the trends and urges the city's operators and service providers to uplift their cyber resilience. To properly focus the cybersecurity investment and operations, it is imperative to realize how the threats jeopardize the business continuity of smart cities.

However, a lack of visibility into real-time cyber incidents-related data makes it problematic to quantify the impact of cyber-attacks. This section outlined numerous real-world cyber incidents in smart city realms, inspected four categories of cyber threats, and linked them to the cyber-attacks and potential impact. The analysis of publicly reported cyber incidents affecting smart cities' infrastructure provides practical insights into cyber threats and vulnerabilities. Nowadays, smart city infrastructure defense is a critical concern. It will grow as the Internet of Things (IoT) increases its induction, and more Industrial Control Systems (ICSs) have been connected to the network.

References

1. Naef Bin Ahmed Al-Saud. A Saudi outlook for cybersecurity strategies extrapolated from western experience. *Joint Force Quarterly*, (64):75, 2012.
2. Zachry Basnight, Jonathan Butts, Juan Lopez, and Thomas Dube. Firmware modification attacks on programmable logic controllers. *International Journal of Critical Infrastructure Protection*, 6(2):76–84, 2013.
3. BBC. Dallas Warning Sirens 'Set off by Hacker'. https://www.bbc.com/news/technology-39552471. Accessed: 2020-04-15.
4. Elisa Bertino and Nayeem Islam. Botnets and internet of things security. *Computer*, 50(2):76–79, 2017.

5. Elias Bou-Harb, Mourad Debbabi, and Chadi Assi. A novel cyber security capability: Inferring Internet-scale infections by correlating malware and probing activities. *Computer Networks*, 94:327–343, 2016.
6. BSI. The state of it security in Germany 2014 - BSI. Accessed: 2022-03-03.
7. Defense Use Case. Analysis of the cyber attack on the Ukrainian power grid. *Electricity Information Sharing and Analysis Center (E-ISAC)*, 388, 2016.
8. CISA. Alert (AA21-287A). Ongoing Cyber Threats to U.S. Water and Wastewater Systems., October 2021. Publication Title: Cybersecurity and Infrastructure Security Agency CISA.
9. Anthony H Cordesman. *Saudi Arabia: National security in a troubled region*. ABC-CLIO, 2009.
10. Ang Cui, Michael Costello, and Salvatore J Stolfo. When firmware modifications attack: A case study of embedded exploitation. In *NDSS*, 2013.
11. INC DRAGOS. Covellite, Aug 2021.
12. Renee Dudley and Daniel Golden. The colonial pipeline ransomware hackers had a secret weapon: self-promoting cybersecurity firms, 2021.
13. Zakir Durumeric, David Adrian, Ariana Mirian, Michael Bailey, and J Alex Halderman. A search engine backed by Internet-wide scanning. In *Proceedings of the 22nd ACM SIGSAC Conference on Computer and Communications Security*, pages 542–553. ACM, 2015.
14. Vincent J Ercolani, Mark W Patton, and Hsinchun Chen. Shodan visualized. In *2016 IEEE Conference on Intelligence and Security Informatics (ISI)*, pages 193–195. IEEE, 2016.
15. Mario Galluscio, Nataliia Neshenko, Elias Bou-Harb, Yongliang Huang, Nasir Ghani, Jorge Crichigno, and Georges Kaddoum. A first empirical look on internet-scale exploitations of IoT devices. In *2017 IEEE 28th Annual International Symposium on Personal, Indoor, and Mobile Radio Communications (PIMRC)*, pages 1–7. IEEE, 2017.
16. Miguel Garcia, Alysson Bessani, and Nuno Neves. Lazarus: Automatic management of diversity in BFT systems. In *Proceedings of the 20th International Middleware Conference*, pages 241–254, 2019.
17. Kyriakos Georgiou, Samuel Xavier-de Souza, and Kerstin Eder. The IoT energy challenge: A software perspective. *IEEE Embedded Systems Letters*, 10(3):53–56, 2017.
18. Samuel Gibbs. Ransomware attack on San Francisco public transit gives everyone a free ride. https://www.theguardian.com/technology/2016/nov/28/passengers-free-ride-san-francisco-muni-ransomeware. Accessed: 2020-04-25.
19. Andy Greenberg. *Sandworm: A new era of cyberwar and the hunt for the Kremlin's most dangerous hackers*. Anchor, 2019.
20. Christopher Helman. The world's biggest oil companies. *Forbes. com*, 16, 2012.
21. Martin Husák, Nataliia Neshenko, Morteza Safaei Pour, Elias Bou-Harb, and Pavel Čeleda. Assessing internet-wide cyber situational awareness of critical sectors. In *Proceedings of the 13th International Conference on Availability, Reliability and Security*, pages 1–6, 2018.
22. DRAGOS INC. New ICS threat activity group: Kamacite, Apr 2021. Accessed: 2022-03-03.
23. Rabia Khan, Pardeep Kumar, Dushantha Nalin K Jayakody, and Madhusanka Liyanage. A survey on security and privacy of 5G technologies: Potential solutions, recent advancements and future directions. *IEEE Communications Surveys & Tutorials*, 2019.
24. K. Kraszewski. SamSam and the Silent Battle of Atlanta. In *2019 11th International Conference on Cyber Conflict (CyCon)*, volume 900, pages 1–16, 2019.
25. M Kumar. DDoS Attack takes down central heating system amidst winter in Finland. https://thehackernews.com/2016/11/heating-system-hacked.html, 2016. Accessed: 2020-04-04.
26. Henry K. Lee. Man pleads guilty to attempted shutdown of state's power grid, Feb 2012. Accessed: 2022-03-03.
27. Gaoqi Liang, Junhua Zhao, Fengji Luo, Steven R Weller, and Zhao Yang Dong. A review of false data injection attacks against modern power systems. *IEEE Transactions on Smart Grid*, 8(4):1630–1638, 2016.
28. Philippe Lin, Morton Swimmer, Akira Urano, Stephen Hilt, and Rainer Vosseler. Securing smart cities. http://branden.biz/wp-content/uploads/2017/06/wp-securing-smart-cities.pdf. Accessed: 2020-04-20.

29. Yao Liu, Peng Ning, and Michael K Reiter. False data injection attacks against state estimation in electric power grids. *ACM Transactions on Information and System Security (TISSEC)*, 14(1):1–33, 2011.
30. Eversheds Sutherland (US) LLP. The cyber incident reporting for critical infrastructure act of 2022. https://www.jdsupra.com/legalnews/the-cyber-incident-reporting-for-6058324/. Accessed: 2022-05-09.
31. Sean Lyngaas. How the Biden administration plans to protect your water systems from hackers, January 2022.
32. Y. Mehmood, F. Ahmad, I. Yaqoob, A. Adnane, M. Imran, and S. Guizani. Internet-of-Things-Based Smart Cities: Recent Advances and Challenges. *IEEE Communications Magazine*, 55(9):16–24, September 2017.
33. Katie Mettler. *Somebody keeps hacking these Dallas road signs with messages about Donald Trump, Bernie Sanders and Harambe the gorilla*. WP Company, March 2019.
34. Savita Mohurle and Manisha Patil. A brief study of WannaCry threat: Ransomware attack 2017. *International Journal of Advanced Research in Computer Science*, 8(5), 2017.
35. NCSC. Supply chain attack examples. Accessed: 2022-03-03.
36. Nataliia Neshenko, Elias Bou-Harb, Jorge Crichigno, Georges Kaddoum, and Nasir Ghani. Demystifying IoT security: an exhaustive survey on IoT vulnerabilities and a first empirical look on internet-scale IoT exploitations. *IEEE Communications Surveys & Tutorials*, 21(3):2702–2733, 2019.
37. Nataliia Neshenko, Martin Husák, Elias Bou-Harb, Pavel Čeleda, Sameera Al-Mulla, and Claude Fachkha. Data-Driven Intelligence for Characterizing Internet-scale IoT Exploitations. In *2018 IEEE Globecom Workshops (GC Wkshps)*, pages 1–7. IEEE, 2018.
38. PALO ALTO NETWORKS. Impacts of Cyberattacks on IoT Devices. https://www.sdxcentral.com/wp-content/uploads/2019/10/iot-research-paper-v4_final.pdf. Accessed: 2020-04-04.
39. Mark Patton, Eric Gross, Ryan Chinn, Samantha Forbis, Leon Walker, and Hsinchun Chen. Uninvited connections: a study of vulnerable devices on the internet of things (IoT). In *2014 IEEE joint intelligence and security informatics conference*, pages 232–235. IEEE, 2014.
40. Nicole Perlroth. Cyberattack on Saudi oil firm disquiets us. *The New York Times*, 24, 2012.
41. Pavel Polityuk. Ukraine to probe suspected Russian cyber attack on grid. https://www.reuters.com/article/us-ukraine-crisis-malware/ukraine-to-probe-suspected-russian-cyber-attack-on-grid-idUSKBN0UE0ZZ20151231, Dec 2015.
42. Kevin Poulsen. Slammer worm crashed Ohio nuke plant net. *The Register*, 20, 2003.
43. PricewaterhouseCoopers. Cyber threat intelligence.
44. A. Rajan, J. Jithish, and S. Sankaran. Sybil attack in IoT: Modelling and defenses. In *2017 International Conference on Advances in Computing, Communications and Informatics (ICACCI)*, pages 2323–2327, Sept 2017.
45. Reuters. Atlanta officials reveal worsening effects of cyber attack. https://www.reuters.com/article/us-usa-cyber-atlanta-budget/atlanta-officials-reveal-worsening-effects-of-cyber-attack-idUSKCN1J231M?feedType=RSS&feedName=technologyNews, 2018. Accessed: 2022-03-01.
46. Robles Frances and Perlroth Nicole. 'Dangerous Stuff': Hackers Tried to Poison Water Supply of Florida Town. *The New York Times*, February 2021.
47. Esther Shein. Incident of the week: Cyber criminals launch ransomware attack on water utility in hurricane ravaged n.c., Oct 2018.
48. Sapalo Sicato, Jose Costa, Pradip Kumar Sharma, Vincenzo Loia, and Jong Hyuk Park. VPNFilter malware analysis on cyber threat in smart home Network. *Applied Sciences*, 9(13):2763, 2019.
49. Jill Slay and Michael Miller. Lessons learned from the Maroochy water breach. In *International conference on critical infrastructure protection*, pages 73–82. Springer, 2007.

50. TOI staff, Amy Spiro, Tobias Siegal, Tobias Siegal staff, TOI, Lazar Berman, Lazar Berman Keller-Lynn, Carrie, TOI staff Keller-Lynn, Carrie, Amy Spiro, Jamey Keaten, TOI staff Agencies, , and et al. Cyber attacks again hit Israel's water system, shutting agricultural pumps, Jul 2020.
51. Wade Trappe, Richard Howard, and Robert S Moore. Low-energy security: Limits and opportunities in the Internet of things. *IEEE Security & Privacy*, 13(1):14–21, 2015.
52. Muhammad Usama, Muhammad Asim, Siddique Latif, Junaid Qadir, and others. Generative Adversarial Networks for Launching and Thwarting Adversarial Attacks on Network Intrusion Detection Systems. In *2019 15th International Wireless Communications & Mobile Computing Conference (IWCMC)*, pages 78–83. IEEE, 2019.
53. Liesbet Van Zoonen. Privacy concerns in smart cities. *Government Information Quarterly*, 33(3):472–480, 2016.
54. B Verizon. Data breach digest. scenarios from the field, 2016.
55. Giovanni Vigna and Richard A Kemmerer. Netstat: A network-based intrusion detection approach. In *Proceedings 14th Annual Computer Security Applications Conference (Cat. No. 98EX217)*, pages 25–34. IEEE, 1998.
56. Onslow Water and Sewer Authority | Official Website. Onslow water and sewer authority: Official website.
57. Jacob Wurm, Khoa Hoang, Orlando Arias, Ahmad-Reza Sadeghi, and Yier Jin. Security analysis on consumer and industrial IoT devices. In *2016 21st Asia and South Pacific Design Automation Conference (ASP-DAC)*, pages 519–524. IEEE, 2016.
58. Aaron Zimba, Zhaoshun Wang, and Mwenge Mulenga. Cryptojacking injection: A paradigm shift to cryptocurrency-based web-centric internet attacks. *Journal of Organizational Computing and Electronic Commerce*, 29(1):40–59, 2019.

Part II
Cyber Situational Awareness for Smart City

> *Ponder and deliberate before you make a move.*
> — **Sun Tzu**

Chapter 3
Cyber Situational Awareness Frontiers

Cyber situational awareness is a vital component of a holistic view of cybersecurity. This chapter puts forward a new perspective on sustained cyber situational awareness for smart cities. It explores the methods that build a foundation for analytics-driven cyber situational awareness at different levels.

Section 3.1 defines the data-driven situational awareness and introduces its frontiers. In Sect. 3.1.2, this chapter explores monitoring and attack detection methods to support the perception level of cyber awareness. Section 3.1.4 examines risk assessment methods and contextualized threat intelligence, which enable the characterization and anticipation of advanced and coordinated threats via assessing their possibilities and impact. In Sect. 3.1.7, this chapter explores the strategies that model dependencies among smart cities' components to project how threats affect the entire ecosystem. Finally, Sect. 3.3 concludes the chapter and highlights key findings.

3.1   Toward Analytics-Driven Situational Awareness

Situational awareness is defined at three levels: *perception, comprehension*, and *projection*, as illustrated in Fig. 3.1 [17].

In the context of cybersecurity, *perception* is defined as system monitoring and intrusion detection. *Comprehension* refers to the understanding of the situation and can be defined by modeling cyber threats or deriving cyber threat intelligence. Lastly, *projection* is an activity of forecasting the future state of a cybersecurity situation and can be accommodated by the methods that model dependency among various components of a smart city.

Moving toward analytics-driven cyber situational awareness, its frontiers are defined as follows (Fig. 3.2):

© The Author(s), under exclusive license to Springer Nature Switzerland AG 2022
N. Neshenko et al., *Smart Cities: Cyber Situational Awareness to Support Decision Making*, https://doi.org/10.1007/978-3-031-18464-2_3

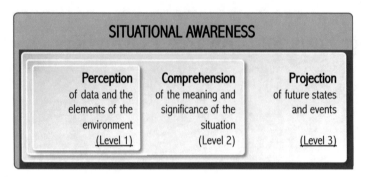

Fig. 3.1 Levels of situational awareness

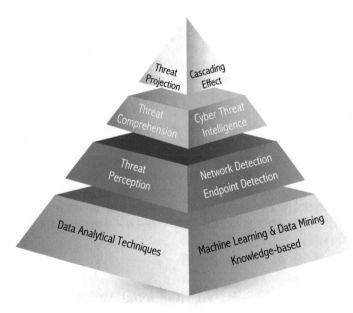

Fig. 3.2 Frontiers of cyber situational awareness

- **Data analytical techniques** represent a basis for analytics-driven cyber situational awareness. This frontier considers machine learning and data mining techniques and knowledge-based methods.
- **Perception frontier** considers network detection and endpoint detection data-driven approaches.
- **Comprehension frontier** takes care of the analytics-driven cyber threat intelligence and risk analysis.
- **Projection frontier** focuses on the methods of modeling dependencies among different components to model a cascading effect of cyber incidents.

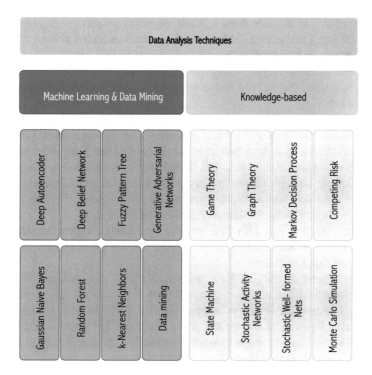

Fig. 3.3 The categories of data analysis techniques employed in the context of cyber situational awareness for smart cities

3.1.1 Data Analytical Techniques

This section briefly overviews relevant data analysis techniques employed in the context of cyber situational awareness of smart cities. It distinguishes two classes, namely (i) machine learning and data mining and (ii) knowledge-based models. The first class consists of methods that derive complex pattern matching capabilities from the training data, including a learning stage. The second class consists of methods that require creating a knowledge base that reflects a system or a security profile. These classes, along with their subclasses, are shown in Fig. 3.3.

3.1.1.1 Machine Learning and Data Mining Methods

Deep autoencoder (DAE) is a feed-forward multi-layer neural network that is trained to compress and reconstruct input data with a minimal difference between input and output [22]. $\bar{X} = D(E(X))$, where X and $\bar{X}$ are input and output, respectively, E is an encoder from the input to the hidden layer, and D is a decoder from the hidden layer to the output. Indeed, a DAE is designed to prioritize the features of X that should be copied to $\bar{X}$. Therefore, it learns important properties of the underlying data. Additionally, the goal of DAE can be formalized as the following optimization problem: $min_{D,E} \| X - D(E(X))$.

Deep Belief Networks (DBNs) [25] consist of multiple layers of stochastic and latent variables and can be regarded as a special form of the Bayesian probabilistic generative model.

Convolutional Neural Network (CNN) [3] is a type of deep, feed-forward neural network usually used to analyze visual representations. A conventional CNN model comprises an input layer, an output layer, and hidden layers. The hidden layers may have different activation functions that include but are not limited to a convolution, Rectified Linear Unit (ReLU) activation, pooling, and fully connected layers. The CNNs can develop internal representations of visual forms. This characteristic unlocks CNN's suitability for data with spatial correlations.

Fast fuzzy pattern tree [50] is a tree-like structure in which the inner nodes are fuzzy logic arithmetic operators and the leaf nodes are associated with fuzzy predicates on input attribute.

Gaussian Naive Bayes is a Bayesian network with one root node that represents the class and n leaf nodes that represent the attributes. The Naïve Bayes classifier is defined as $N(a) = argmax_{c \in C} P(c) \prod_{i=1}^{n} P(x_i \mid c)$, where $a = X_1 = x_1, \ldots, X_n = x_n$ is a complete set of attributes. In Gaussian Naive Bayes, each attribute is defined by a Gaussian probability density function (PDF) as $X_i \sim N(\mu, \sigma^2)(x) = \frac{1}{\sqrt{(2\pi\sigma^2)}} e^{-\frac{(x-\mu)^2}{2\sigma^2}}$, where μ is the mean and σ^2 is the variance.

Random Forest Classifier is a machine learning method that leverages decision trees and ensemble learning. Indeed, the forests are a collection of tree-structured classifiers $h(x, \Theta_k), k = 1, ..$, where Θ_k are independent identically distributed random vectors and each tree is assigned a vote for the most popular class at input x. In fact, the prediction can be made based on majority voting or weighted voting. Additionally, Random Forests can use a large number of attributes and therefore do not require feature selection. Another advantage of this classifier is its resistance to over-fitting. However, it heavily depends on the implemented random generator and is deficient in model interpretability. *k-Nearest Neighbors* is a popular machine learning method that does not have a learning phase but instead memorizes the training data. Indeed, to predict the class of an unseen instance, the KNN classifier measures the similarity between data points by using the Euclidean distance $d(x, y) = \sqrt{(\sum_{k=1}^{n} (x_k - y_k)^2)}$, where x_k and y_k are featured elements of instances x and y, respectively.

3.1.1.2 Knowledge-Based Models

Graph theory. In a cybersecurity setting, graphs can describe attack prerequisites (vulnerabilities) or attack pathways. The algorithm of finding the shortest path in the tree determines the system exploitability index or optimal route of attack from the attacker's standpoint. In fact, complementing the above graphs with countermeasures aids defense prioritization.

Game theory is the mathematical modeling of interactions among agents. The formal theory defines a game as $Game = (P_i, S, s, \pi_i)$, where P_i stands for players $(i = 1, 2, \ldots)$, S is a set of pure strategies for each player I, $s : S_1 S_2$ is a set of pure strategy profile, and $\pi_i : S \rightarrow R$ is the players' payoff functions. Furthermore, the solution to a game is represented as optimal decisions of the players, who may have mutual or conflicting interests.

Markov decision process (MDP) is a stochastic process that is defined as a tuple (S, A, P_a, R_a), where S is a finite set of states, A is a finite state of actions, P_a is the probability that action a in state s at the time t will lead state $s\prime$ at time $t + 1$, and R_a is a reward expected to be received after transition from state s to $s\prime$ due to action a. Moreover, the outcome of MDP is a policy π that maps each state to an action a taken in this state s. Additionally, the process has an important property; the action only depends on the current state, not on the prior history. Furthermore, the policy may be realized through a lookup table or may involve extensive computation [16].

State Machine is an abstract model that represents how the output is computed based on the input. Indeed, the model is formulated mathematically as $SM = (\Sigma, S, s_0, \sigma, F)$, where Σ is a finite set of symbols, S is a finite set of states, s_0 is an initial state of S, σ is a state transition function $\sigma : S \rightarrow \Sigma \rightarrow S$, and F is a finite set of final states.

Stochastic Activity Networks (SANs) are used for performance and dependability evaluations. As a stochastic extension of Petri nets, SAN consists of the following elements: places, gates, and activities. Indeed, the gates connect places to activities (input gates) and activities to places (output gates). Additionally, the activities can be instantaneous and timed, which have the delay to completion. Moreover, formally, $SAN = ((P, A, I, O, \gamma, \tau, \iota, o), \mu_0, C, F, G)$, where P is a finite state of places, A is a finite state of activities, I is a finite state of input gates, O is a finite state of output gates, γ is a number of cases for each activity, τ specifies the type of activity, ι maps input gates to activities, and o maps the output gates to places.

Stochastic Well-formed Nets (SWNs) [12] is a system model that captures the main characteristics of complex systems with the large number of interconnected components. Mathematically, it is defined as $SWN = (WN, \theta)$, where WN is a well-formed colored Petri net and θ is a function of transitions.

Competing Risk Theory [13] assesses a specific risk in the complex presence of other k risks and attempts to predict the consequences of removing this risk.

Monte Carlo Simulation is a mathematical method of generating random variables for risk or uncertainty modeling of a certain system.

Table 3.1 maps the data analytics techniques with further reviewed data-driven methods for cyber situational awareness.

Sections 3.1.2–3.1.7[1] showcase the methods employed at the different levels of cyber situational awareness.

---

[1] These sections are partially adopted from [42].

Table 3.1 Mapping of data analysis techniques and reviewed methods

Data analysis technique	Level 1: Perception	Level 2: Comprehension	Level 3: Projection
Deep autoencoder (DAE)	[36]		
Deep Belief Networks (DBNs)	[23]		
Convolutional Network	[6]		
Fuzzy Pattern Tree	[14]		
Generative Adversarial Networks (GANs)	[34]		
Gaussian Naive Bayes	[29]		
Random Forest classifier	[29]		
k-Nearest Neighbors	[7, 29]	[4, 39]	
Graph theory		[28, 35, 52, 54, 57]	[20, 26, 30, 32, 55, 56]
Game theory			[20]
Markov decision process/chain		[38]	[30]
State Machine			[10, 24, 43]
Stochastic Activity Networks (SANs)			[9, 10, 43]
Stochastic Well-formed Nets (SWNs)			[9]
Competing Risks Theory			[10]
Monte Carlo Simulation			[10]
Various data mining methods	[46]	[11, 15, 19, 27, 45, 47, 58]	

3.1.2 Threat Perception: Attack Detection Methods

Regular threat assessment, though extremely valuable and insightful, cannot capture all possible threat capabilities. To this end, a retrospective incident analysis captures several threat attributes and system characteristics, which allows the measurement of the effectiveness of the implemented defense mechanisms. Indeed, scientific efforts toward the development of compelling techniques for the detection of threats and malicious events have been studied for decades, yielding a plethora of inference methods. A recent trend continues to converge toward machine learning techniques, which addresses the problem of recognizing malicious patterns in (network) data flows/traffic to infer anomalies.

In this vein, the main goal of the work conducted by Oza et al. [45] is to detect replay attacks—a subset of false data injection attacks—in an effort to secure traffic lights. Indeed, such attacks minimize the efficiency of traffic management systems and potentially can introduce life-threatening situations. To this end, the authors simulated a replay attack and studied existing detection mechanisms. They identified several shortcomings in these mechanisms and offered a threshold-based method for detecting an attack. Additionally, the authors determined a threshold by analyzing the occupancy's sensors' readings with and without attacks. The detection algorithm observes the occupancy's sensor's data over time and alarms the operator if the change is above a defined threshold.

To detect energy theft, He et al. [23] attempted to identify potential malicious injections in the context of a power grid. The authors proposed a real-time scheme for capturing the behavioral features of false data injection attacks. Indeed, the architecture of the solution consists of a State Vector Estimator (SVE) and a Conditional Deep Belief Network (CDBN). The latter consists of a Conditional Gaussian–Bernoulli RBM method at the first hidden layer and a conventional RBM technique at all remaining hidden layers. Additionally, the CDBN is responsible for the extraction of high-dimensional temporal features. Moreover, the SVE evaluates the quality of the measurement data by calculating the l_2-norm of residual measurement and compares the calculation result η with the predetermined threshold τ. Further, when $\eta > \tau$, the measurement is considered to be compromised.

The infrastructure of smart cities, particularly those aspects dealing with IoT devices, can be infected by malware or recruited into botnets for conducting DDoS attacks and other coordinated events. To this end, Azmoodeh et al. [6] applied a convolution network to the vector representation of Operations Codes (OpCodes) to detect IoT malware. The model first generates the graph of OpCodes and then converts it to eigenspace (i.e., eigenvector and eigenvalue) in order to pass it as an input to a convolutional network.

Furthermore, Dovom et al. [14] proposed a malware classification technique rooted in fuzzy and fast fuzzy pattern tree that were applied to a vector representation of OpCodes sequences. In a nutshell, a fuzzy pattern classifier is a collection of fuzzy pattern trees and each PT_i is a pattern tree associated with class. The tree that produces a higher score is then used to assign the class. In fact, the authors leveraged a class-wise information gain to select the most beneficial features for flow graph generation. Additionally, the proposed method outperformed SVM, KNN, Random Forest, and Decision Tree classifiers. Moreover, the proposed method demonstrated a general potential in interacting with noise and ambiguity, making it a considerable solution for deployment at the edge of a network.

Malicious behaviors of recruited IoT devices (into botnets) can be detected in different stages of the attacks. Along this line of thought, Kumar et al. [29] endeavored to detect individual bots before an actual attack, i.e., during the scanning phase. Indeed, they analyzed network activities for early detection of individual bots. Toward this, several machine learning algorithms, such as Random Forest, KNN, and Gaussian Naive Bayes, were used to label the network traffic that demonstrates a behavior similar to an IoT-botnet behavior. To increase the performance of the method, the authors operated on an aggregate traffic in order to detect an IoT access gateway level. This method was proved to be faster and reduced the memory space required.

Alternatively, since some attackers made successful attempts to avoid detection, it is crucial to be able to detect the infections in later stages of the attack. To this end, Meidan et al. [36] proposed N-BaIoT, a network-based approach that detects compromised IoT devices that are used to launch attacks. The approach extracts statistical features that capture the behavior of the network and uses deep autoencoders (DAE) in order to detect anomalous network traffic generated by compromised IoT devices. The method was proven to be able to detect previously unseen botnets with low rates of false alarms, which is crucial for resource allocation.

In an alternative work, Alazab et al. [46] proposed a detection technique that semantically discriminates botnets and verifies the behavioral legitimacy of numerous smart city's IoT-based applications. Indeed, the authors leveraged the domain name system's (DNS) services to build upon a framework that initially visualizes DNS features (such as domain name length, domain name entropy, and domain name n-gram). Consequently, the method estimates a similarity score and compares it with a predefined threshold. The domain names that did not pass the threshold are labeled as spoofed. Additionally, a cost-sensitive deep learning algorithm analyzes other domains. Here, the results are also visualized for the administrator for easy of digestion.

Alternatively, Raza et al. [48] proposed a method to detect attacks inside the 6LoWPAN network protocol, which is actively used in smart lighting solutions. By observing a network topology, the framework's modules grasp inconsistencies in node communications and detect attacks. First, the approach gathers information about the network to reconstruct a Destination-Oriented Directed Acyclic Graph (DODAG). Then, it infuses the node's parent and neighbor information into the graph. An algorithm that analyzes consistency in a network graph carries the detection of false data injection and routing attacks. In an extended version [53], the authors leveraged Expected Transmissions (ETX) metrics, which are measured by sending periodical probe packets between the participating neighbors.

By modeling nonlinear correlation among multiple time series, Li et al. [33] designed an unsupervised GAN-based anomaly detection (GAN-AD) method for inferring attacks in multi-process CPS with various network sensors and actuators. The proposed GAN employed Long Short-Term Recurrent Neural Networks (LSTM-RNNs) for both the generator and the discriminator and calculated scores to indicate the level of abnormality in the time series. In fact, when tested on the CPS dataset from the Secure Water Treatment Testbed (SwaT), the model demonstrated that it outperformed existing unsupervised detection methods.

Alternatively, to detect crypto-ransomware in IoT networks, Azmoodeh et al. [7] classified power usage patterns on IoT nodes and discriminated ransomware-infected nodes. At the first stage, the methodology recorded a sequence of energy usage for each process of the targeted devices, followed by a calculation of the distance that measures an optimal alignment between two time-dependent sequences known as dynamic time warping (DTW). Finally, the authors employed three classifiers, namely Neural Network, SVM, and KNN. In combination with dynamic time warping, KNN outperformed other classifiers and demonstrated remarkable performance (94.27%) in detecting ransomware in the IoT nodes.

One of the biggest cybersecurity concerns directly refers to the inability of machine learning methods to combat adversarial attacks. Indeed, the proactive data-driven defense methods that aim to cope with the attack against machine learning algorithms propose to sanitize the training and testing data by detecting the adversarial injection. For instance, Baracaldo et al. [8] leveraged provenance data, which consists of meta-data describing the origin and lineage of each data point, in order to identify malicious manipulation of the training data. Additionally, the authors pinpointed generated poisoned data and formed provenance data. Moreover, the validation unveiled that employing this method as a filter during the training phase significantly improves classification performance.

Furthermore, the framework proposed by Laishram and Phoha [31] clusters the feature space of the input and filters out suspicious data points. The method calculates an average distance of each data point from the other points in the same cluster. It then considers a class label as an additional feature with a proper weight. Additionally, the data points with a confidence level less than 95% are removed from the training data to achieve input purity. Moreover, empirical experiments demonstrated remarkable accuracy improvement of the SVM classifier.

3.1.3 Evaluation Metrics

The following metrics evaluate the performance of the reviewed models. The first one refers to the ability of the model to classify the instances correctly, while the second one measures how well the model can capture data patterns. The next metric looks at the transparency of the model or how well the process is considered trustworthy. A final metric analyzes the capability of the approach to capture the attributes of the detected threats. The ability of the method to label instances can be presented as *accuracy, precision, recall,* and *F-measure.* Indeed, the estimation of these measures depends on the following indicators.

- True positive *(tp)* indicates that the positive instance is correctly classified.
- True negative *(tn)* implies that the negative instance is correctly labeled.
- False positive *(fp)* indicates that the negative instance is misclassified as positive.
- False negative *(fn)* indicates that the positive instance is misclassified as negative.

Accuracy is considered to be a prime indicator of the correctness of the detection model. It is calculated as the percentage of all the correctly classified instances to all instances as $(tp + tn) / (tp + tn + fp + fn)$. However, the accuracy can be misleading in case of high class imbalance [60]. In this case, the following metrics are required to evaluate a model.

Precision measures the proportion of correctly classified instances of all the records that are classified as positive. It is defined as $tp / (tp + fp)$. Indeed, a low precision can indicate a large number of fp.

Recall, also known as sensitivity or true positive rate, represents the ratio of correctly classified positive instances to a number of instances that should be classified as positive. It is formally defined as $tp / (tp + fn)$. In fact, a low recall indicates a large number of fn.

F-Measure is the harmonic mean of precision and recall. It is defined as $(2 * tp) / (2 * tp + fp + fn)$.

The problem with the ability of the model to classify instances correctly is that it does not validate the model's performance on previously unseen data. To this end, evaluation of how well the model captures the data pattern can be instrumental. For instance, following methods generalize a model's performance and help evaluate a model's ability to capture data patterns.

- *Hold-out* technique randomly divides the dataset into two subsets, namely, training and testing. The split is usually 60/40, 70/30, or 80/20. To avoid a situation when the uneven distribution of classes is found in a subset, it is essential to balance the instances belonging to the different classes. k-fold cross validation divides datasets into k subsets; one of them is used as the testing set and the other k-1 subsets form the training set. Indeed, the method ensures that each instance is a part of a testing set exactly one time. Additionally, the process of training and testing the model is repeated k times and the average error through all tests is used for evaluation. However, the k-fold cross validation is computationally expensive, because the training and testing process should be repeated k times.
- *Leave-one-out* cross validation is a k-fold cross validation with k equal to the number of data instances in the dataset. The evaluation produced by this method is considered to be good even though it is not optimal in terms of computation.
- *Matthews correlation coefficient (MCC)* measure considers all metrics from the confusion matrix to diminish the influence of one class.
  $$MCC = \frac{tp*tn - fp*fn}{\sqrt{(tp+fp)(tp+fn)(tn+fp)(tn+fn)}}.$$ Indeed, MCC equal to 1 indicates the perfect prediction, while -1 refers to the worst prediction.

Furthermore, users criticize machine learning models as black-box due to the lack of interpretability that helps them understand how the models make decisions based on the data.

A look at how the model quantifies the influence of each input, details the model's errors, and records the results at each step of the process helps evaluate model transparency. Indeed, with different levels of detail, several works visually explained the actions of the proposed methods. However, nearly 50% of the reviewed data-driven strategies are still obscure. The clarity of the model can boost trust and practical adoption; therefore, the authors should give more explanation to the interpretability of the results and the process itself. Table 3.2 summarizes the metrics presented in the reviewed works for detection methods. Although this chapter reports the value of various metrics for each work, they are hardly comparable due to the underlying nature of the datasets used for evaluation and the different detail levels provided in the reviewed papers.

The numerous models achieved accuracy over 95%. Additionally, the validation methods and used datasets demonstrated a profound effect on accuracy. For instance, the majority of techniques that used artificial datasets or simulated environments reported lower accuracy than their peers that leveraged live data. In fact, the 10-fold cross validation exhibited higher accuracy.

Let us take a look at the explicit outcomes of the detection methods and measure how these outcomes answer the following questions:

- *etection goal*: what kind of attack does the method attempt to detect?
- *Attack phase:* at what phase of attack the method detects an intrusion?
- *Attack vector:* does the method analyze how the attack was facilitated?
- *Attribution:* does the method attribute the attack to a specific adversary?
- *Time to detection (TTD):* how long does it take to detect an attack?
- *Impact:* does the method analyze potential attack impact?

Table 3.3 summarizes the details that can be extracted from the analyzed methods.

3.1.4 Threat Comprehension: Risk Analysis and Cyber Threat Intelligence

The growing number and scale of cyber threats demand proactive decisions for the development of ample cybersecurity capabilities. In fact, the core challenges for cyber-related decision-making are the uncertainty of cyber threats and their severity and the technological advances that introduce new vulnerabilities. Given the heterogeneity of IoT devices, a myriad of vulnerabilities requires patching and monitoring. Therefore, it is imperative to set the priority to secure critical weaknesses and allocate time and budget effectively. Risk analysis and contextualized cyber threat intelligence capabilities help to discover unknown incidents and attack trends while assessing and comprehending their impacts.

Table 3.2 The performance benchmarks of various attack detection methods

Reference	Accuracy (%)	Precision (%)	Recall (%)	F-Measure	TP	FP	Validation
Oza et al. [45]	–	–	–	–	–	–	–
He et al. [23]	93.73–98.51	–	–	–	–	–	–
Azmoodeh et al. [6]	99.68	98.59	98.37	0.98	–	–	10-fold
Dovom et al. [14]	96.4	94.33	89.71	0.89	–	–	MCC
Kumar et al. [29]	94.44	92	1	0.96	–	–	Hold-out
Meidan et al. [36]	–	–	–	–	100	0.7	Hold-out
R et al. [46]	99	85	99	92	–	–	Hold-out
Raza et al. [48]	80–100	–	100	–	–	–	–
Shreenivas et al. [53]	90–100	–	–	–	–	–	–
Li et al. [34]	94.8	93	63.64	0.75	–	–	Hold-out
Azmoodeh et al. [7]	94.27	89.19	95.65	0.92	–	–	Leave-one-out
Baracaldo et al. [8]	Up to 90	–	–	–	–	–	Hold-out
Laishram & Phoha [31]	Up to 99	–	–	–	–	–	10-fold

Table 3.3 Attack details provided by the detection method

Reference	Detection goal	Attack phase	TTD
Oza et al. [45]	False data injection	Action	
He et al. [23]	False data injection	Installation	
Azmoodeh et al. [6]	Malware	Exploitation	
Dovom et al. [14]	Malware	Exploitation	
Kumar et al. [29]	Probing detection	Reconnaissance	
Meidan et al. [36]	Botnet	Action	174±212 ms
R et al. [46]	Botnet	Action	
Raza et al. [48]	Routing attacks	Action	
	False data injection		
Shreenivas et al. [53]	Routing attacks	Action	
Li et al. [34]	Anomaly	Various	
Azmoodeh et al. [7]	Anomaly	Various	
Baracaldo et al. [8]	Ransomware (IoT)	Exploitation	
Laishram & Phoha [31]	Poisoning attack	Exploitation	

3.1.5 Risk Analysis

In the context of risk assessment, Li et al. [35] estimated cybersecurity risk in traffic light systems. The authors first employed a game-theoretic framework to determine the worst-case traffic management performance under attack. The metric is then used to determine the severity of a particular attack as $S_i = P_0 - P_I$, where P_0 represents a system performance that is not under an attack and P_i^* represents a system performance under an attack. The researchers then determined a cybersecurity risk of a traffic light system under a certain traffic network condition by calculating it as $R = \sum_{i \in C} L_i * S_i$. Furthermore, a cyber-risk mitigation framework is formulated using subjective decision rule known as a minimax-regret criterion. Here, the regret is defined as the risk under a specific traffic condition with no countermeasures employed. Additionally, the ranked countermeasures manage to minimize the worst-case regret.

Kelarestaghi et al. [27] conducted a vulnerability-oriented risk assessment by employing a National Institute of Standards and Technology (NIST) risk model. The authors synthesized real-world misdemeanors and research publications that study the attacks against in-vehicle network vulnerabilities in order to quantify the potential impact of the exploitations. Safety, operational, and security issues were then mapped into a visual matrix to facilitate risk prioritization. Moreover, an empirical study unveiled the severe impact of cyber-attacks on the safety, security, and operation of the vehicle.

In an alternative work, Kotzanikolaou et al. [28] assessed a possible cascading effect of a single incident on multiple CIs. In fact, the approach models the connections between infrastructure as a graph where the edges represent the dependencies under regular operation. Additionally, the method does not differentiate the risks but uses the impact of adverse effects as a result of a risk assessment for each infrastructure.

It is hard to overestimate the importance of IoT in a smart city's ecosystem. Given the diversity of IoT devices, the vulnerabilities of the entire system are countless [41]. Sicari at al. [54] proposed a general-purpose risk assessment methodology in the context of IoT deployment. The framework first identifies the model's components and forms an attack tree with the nodes representing a different way of attacks and the leaves symbolizing the vulnerabilities v_i. Indeed, each vulnerability is associated with an exploitability level E_i. The latter indicates a measure of how probable the v_i is exploited to perform the attack. In the next step, the framework models a graph to depict the dependencies d_i among v_i. The exploitability level is then assigned to each edge of the graph and is updated according to the formula $E_{(i+1)} = max(E_0(v_i)), min(E(d_i)), E_i(E_i)))$, which indicates the risk of exploitation. Moreover, the approach enables scalability in terms of effortless adding or removing components from the framework.

Furthermore, Wang et al. [57] proposed a vulnerability assessment method rooted in an attribute attack graph. In fact, the model takes a network topology, the vulnerabilities, and an attack graph to generate an optimal attack map. It further calculates max loss from the exploitation by using a score from the Common Vulnerability Scoring System (CVSS) [37]. Finally, the model employs an augmented path algorithm to suggest an attack priority order and determines the weakest link in the system to prioritize their monitoring and security. In a complementary work, Radanliev et al. [47] proposed an economic impact assessment framework for IoT. The authors adopted the Cyber Value at Risk model to measure the maximum possible loss over a given time period and the MicroMort model to predict uncertainty through units of mortality risk.

Nazeeruddin [38] leveraged Markov's decision process in order to model the security of smart cities at a high level of abstraction. The model considers the system components and their types (e.g., sensor, actuator, etc.), the cyber-attack against each element, the vulnerabilities with the exploitation probabilities that are extracted from the CVSS database, and the human involvement at the last level of defense. In case the attack successfully passed two levels of defense mechanisms, the model generates an alert for review by security analysts for further investigation. The authors demonstrated that the model could easily be adjusted with vulnerabilities to recalculate the risk level.

Shivraj et al. [52] offered a generic risk assessment framework for IoT systems. The authors described information flow across the different components as a weighted directed acyclic graph $G(V, E)$. The edge E between nodes V indicates a dependency of one node to another. Indeed, one node can be connected to multiple ones, producing numerous connections. Additionally, the value of the edge weight is directly linked to the impact of the attacks. Moreover, various attacks are modeled through attack trees, while their propagation is represented using a bipartite graph. The latter allows capturing nested attacks (e.g., through spoofing an attack on a node; tampering, spoofing, and denial of service attacks can be carried out on its parent node). The authors demonstrated the risk computation based on a simulated system of a connected car.

Mohsin et al. [39] proposed a probabilistic model aiming to automatically assess the likelihood of a threat realization in various IoT system configurations. At the very first stage, the framework leverages a Markov model to represent the system's architecture, security threats, and attackers' capabilities to predict the likelihood of an attack and suggest a secure configuration. Additionally, the framework addresses both concurrent and sequential elements of the system by assigning the synchronization labels for modeling concurrency, flags, and counters for the subsequent flow. Moreover, the framework, dubbed as IoTRiskAnalyzer, answers the question of what the best possible configuration for a security requirement is and how promising it is to enable the diagnostic of a cybersecurity posture.

3.1.6 Cyber Threat Intelligence

One of the core goals of advanced threat detection is to comprehend the discovered malicious event and identify potential threats and trends. In this context, Falco et al. [18] designed a method for automatic identification of attack strategies that can be used to compromise a CCTV network. The approach combines several established frameworks to address the full lifecycle of the attack. Additionally, a Lockheed Martin's cyber kill chain is used to define the sequential phases. Moreover, the Open Web Application Security Project (OWASP) allowed identifying attack surface areas. Furthermore, a MITRE's Common Attack Pattern Enumeration and Classifications (CAPEC) along with Adversarial Tactics, Techniques, and Common Knowledge (ATT&CK) framework defined the required actions to conduct the attack. Finally, Kali Linux tools and known exploit tactics by MITRE's ATT&CK Matrix execute the actions. The result, compared with the manually generated attack tree, demonstrated considerably greater depth and information granularity than the manual tree because it moves through each phase of the cyber kill chain.

Angelini et al. [4] associated network topology and geography with the resultant impact using a visualization based on areas of corruption. This method was used in order to concentrate the attention on the most harmful risk of cyber incidents. In fact, the method's architecture is comprised of several components, including knowledge base generation, attack, risk, and response modeling. First, the model defines business processes of the power distribution system and then assigns the mission priority and the cyber events that can adversely affect the business process. For visualization purposes, the authors clustered dense areas of network nodes and employed the Voronoi diagram to effectively spot the geographical placement. The reported results highlighted the sub-network which could cause mission degradation if compromised.

To analyze the degree of exploitation, Wang et al. [58] measured smart cities threat factors by combining more than 200 gathered features based on a Hardware, intelligence, Software, Policies, and Operation (HiSPO) approach [59]. After assigning a weight $w_i = 1/\sum_i(r_i)$ to each threat, the threat factor was calculated as $t = 0.5 * \sum w_i * (t_i + \delta) + 0.001 * (C_B + C_T + C_E) + 0.02 * f_{TI}$, where C_B, C_T, C_E are base, temporal, and environmental scores in CVSS, respectively. Additionally, an adjusted weight for a threat is denoted as δ, while f_{TI} symbolizes a threat intelligence value. Moreover, the final report produced threat factors that were calculated before mitigation and after the assessment and mitigation period. Furthermore, it showed that the proposed methodology can considerably minimize the risks for smart cities.

In an alternative work, Bou-Harb et al. [11] prototyped an IoT cyber threat intelligence platform for inferring and disclosing Internet-scale compromised IoT devices. To this end, the authors amalgamated the results from passive and active measurements of Internet-wide network traffic analysis. In fact, through an authenticated platform, they disclosed raw data related to numerous compromised IoT devices in diverse sectors, including critical infrastructure. Indeed, the platform estimates the indicators of a highly exploited hosting environment to provide early warnings regarding such exploitations and leverage visual dashboards in order to facilitate threat exploration and prioritization.

Furthermore, honeypots trap an adversary by intentionally creating security vulnerabilities in specific technologies. These devices (or software) record malicious activities so that attack vectors and patterns can be further investigated. Given that ZigBee-based IoT devices are actively used in smart cities settings [40], the honeypot that simulates a ZigBee gateway proposed by Dowling et al. [15] is instrumental to explore attacks against smart cities. After three months of monitoring the activity that has targeted the ZigBee gateway, the researchers reported 6 types of executed attacks. These include dictionary and brute force attacks, scans, botnets, and a number of other independent events. The authors also reported that dictionary attacks represented nearly 94% of all attacks.

One of the most significant challenges of methods discussed above in a smart city's settings is the evaluation of the proposed approach. This issue is confirmed by the absence of standard evaluation metrics in the reviewed literature. Since the selection of risk assessment methodology depends on the system infrastructure, security requirements, and purpose [51], we define herein the following set of metrics to evaluate the sufficiency of each model.

- *Perspective*: this criterion focuses on the resource level that is used to identify the risk. It can be described as three categories: asset-driven, service-driven, and business-driven methods [51]. First, the asset-driven category identifies risks associated with smart cities' assets, such as IIoT and IoT devices, cloud services, or software, to name a few. Second, the service-driven models identify the risk in the smart cities' provided services. For instance, the risk can be assessed for smart transportation. Lastly, the business-driven risk assessment concentrates on the business processes.
- *Application area*: the intertwined architecture of smart cities makes the estimation of an impact way harder than in traditional ICT environments. Indeed, such infrastructure consists of a myriad of heterogeneous devices, communication protocols, and big data ecosystems, not to mention the strong relationship between the elements of the architecture.

- *Cybersecurity scope*: Typically, the cybersecurity scope refers to the impact on main cybersecurity objectives, namely, confidentiality, integrity, availability, and accountability. However, to be consistent with the threats described in "Threat Landscape," we classify the scope based on four previously identified classes: exploratory threats, infrastructure sabotage, data manipulation, and third-party breaches.
- *Threat identification strategy*: we observed two main approaches: manual and automatic. The latter, however, relies on third-party databases or platforms.
- *Uncertainty handling*: we extracted two strategies that the reviewed models employ to handle uncertainty. These are probabilistic and ordinal strategies. Indeed, the widely used probabilistic method has well-defined mathematical properties. Additionally, the ordinal measure is represented by ranking the exploitability level of the attack vector. In fact, this ranking is chosen on a scale of 1–9, where 1 is the most difficult path.
- *Produced outcome*: we observe two main risk calculation methods. Indeed, the framework either computes the exploitability level (not the risk) or employs the classical way that takes into account a likelihood of exploitation and a potential impact indicator. Additionally, the choice of the method that computes risk implies that the models are developed for general purpose. We note that this method omits other angles of risk evaluation such as financial interpretation, risk assessment for compliance, or safety reasons. Although several publications do not directly state the supported decisions, the produced output implies that the safeguard prioritization is a key outcome. In fact, it confirms our previous conclusion that the reviewed methods are general purpose and omit the prioritization of investments and compliance.
- *Credibility*: this criterion measures the ability of the approach to capture the real risk level. Indeed, the credibility of the risk assessment model can be measured as reliability and validity. While the former is concerned with the consistency of the results, validity deals with the resulting accuracy compared to the true underlying risk [5].

Table 3.4 combines the metrics for each selected method and leads to the following remarks. First, the majority of the reviewed methods focus on an asset-based approach, even though the effect on smart cities' operations is still at its infancy. Second, the loss of power due to the exploitation of the power grid can lead to a degradation of the traffic control system's performance. At the same time, the reviewed methods do not take into account this dependency. However, the accurate impact estimation seems to be unconceivable due to the lack of empirical data. Besides, all the methods fail to take into account an emerging risk of using infrastructure as an attack platform [44]. Third, the assessment in the reviewed works centers on infrastructure and data manipulation, with a significant bias to the former class. However, the exploratory and third-party threats are the entry points for many attacks, while risk assessment methods seem to be undervalued (in terms of their significance). Fourth, the reviewed models choose probabilistic and ordinal measures with the nearest frequency, knowing that a game-theoretic approach is

Table 3.4 Evaluation of advanced detection methods. Perspective: A—asset-driven, S—service-driven and B—business-driven. Cybersecurity scope: E—exploratory threat, I—infrastructure sabotage, D—data manipulation, and T—third-party breaches.

Reference	Perspective			Threat enum.	Cybersecurity scope				Uncertainty handling	Basis for prioritization
	A	S	B		E	I	D	T		
Li et al. [35]	✓			Manual			✓		Game-theoretic	Mitigation prioritization
Kelarestaghi et al. [27]		✓		Manual		✓			N/A	Impact assessment
Kotzanikolaou et al. [28]	✓			Manual	N/S				Probabalistic	Mitigation prioritization
Sicari at al. [54]	✓			Manual		✓	✓		Ordinal	Exploitability level
Wang et al. [57]	✓			Manual			✓		Probabalistic	Threat factor
Radanliev et al. [47]	✓			Manual		✓				Economic impact
Mohammad [38]		✓		Manual		✓			Probabalistic	Threat factor
Shivraj et al. [52]	✓			Manual		✓			Ordinal	Threat factor
Mohsin et al. [39]	✓			Manual		✓	✓		Probabalistic	Prioritized configuration
Falco et al. [19]	✓			Automatic		✓			Ordinal	Attack path projection
Angelini et al. [4]			✓	Manual	N/S				Ordinal	Operational impact
Wang et al. [58]			✓	Manual		✓	✓		Probabalistic	Threat factor
Bou-Harb et al. [11]	✓			Automatic		✓			Probabalistic	Situational awareness

rarely explored. Finally, although the reviewed papers seldom measure reliability (in fact, only one model, which is proposed by Falco et al. [19], compared the results with a model produced by experts), all of them omitted the validity measurement.

3.1.7 Threat Projection: Strategies for Modeling Cascading Effect

Heterogeneous communication protocols and shared infrastructure connect various embedded systems to make cities more effective. Additionally, different service providers exchange information and resources to support the sustainable operation of a smart city. This high interdependence introduces a large number of possible attacks and vulnerabilities that directly relate to the severity of the threat and have a multiplicative effect on the prioritization of mitigation. Indeed, a threat that results in the loss of one service or infrastructure can potentially impact other services as they use each other's resources. Moreover, identifying these vulnerabilities and their impact is challenging because of the high complexity of the connection among different infrastructure. Furthermore, each smart city's component has a variety of security requirements which introduces additional challenges.

Any disruption in smart cities' systems would have an impact on its effective operation as well as the safety and well-being of its citizens. Additionally, a formal dependency model of the smart city's elements would uncover insights into fundamental characteristics of the system's topology and could be instrumental in developing its security profile, assessing the cumulative impact of cyber threats, and estimating the effect of countermeasures. While the discussed dependency models do not consider cyber threats, understanding the connection between different domains affects threat prioritization and mitigation.

To this end, Laugé et al. [32] demonstrated how a failure in one service could affect other domains. In this context, the researchers conducted a series of interviews with experts and quantified the magnitude of the adverse effect on dependent services such as energy and connectivity. The results, which include characterization of the time dimension to dynamically study the impact, enabled a deep understanding of direct and higher order dependencies to prioritize mitigation.

Furthermore, König et al. [30] proposed a framework to represent the effect of adverse events in highly coupled critical infrastructures (CIs). The approach modeled the dependencies between infrastructures as a directed graph. In fact, each CI is denoted as a single vertex, while the edges symbolize the reliance on the others CIs' resources. Each edge is then assigned to a class $c \in 1, 2, \ldots C$ which represents a fixed type of inner or mutual dependency. Additionally, these dependencies are assessed using a Markov chain and by leveraging interviews with experts. Moreover, the visualization of dependencies illustrated how the limitations in one CI affect dependent CIs and how this impact changes over time.

To identify the minimum subset of critical infrastructure nodes and select the most rewarding mitigation priorities, Stergiopoulos et al. [55] input a dependency risk graph into their model and define the correlation between centrality metrics and high impact nodes. Furthermore, the authors used centrality metrics to develop and test various risk mitigation strategies that maximize risk reduction. The results demonstrated that centrality measures could characterize critical infrastructure nodes that significantly affect the overall risk in a dependency risk graph.

In an alternative work, Stergiopoulos et al. [56] modeled dependencies among infrastructures as a graph $G = (N, E)$, where N is a set of nodes representing infrastructures or components, and E is a set of edges that symbolize dependencies. In fact, an edge from node CI_i to node CI_{ij}, i.e., $CI_i \rightarrow CI_j$, denotes a risk relation that is derived from the dependence of infrastructure CI_j on a service provided by infrastructure CI_i. This relation is quantified using the impact $I_{(i,j)}$ and the likelihood $L_{(i,j)}$ that a disruption will be realized. Additionally, the cascading resulting risk is represented as a numerical value of each edge. The growth level is then precomputed and is passed to a fuzzy ranking system that provides realistic assessments of the evolution of potential failures.

One of the goals of Beccuti et al. [9] was to investigate the consequences of a malfunctioning communication system when the power grid experienced a failure. To this end, the authors modeled and simulated the electrical state of the Electrical Power System (EPS) using a Stochastic Activity Network (SAN). In contrast, a Denial of Service (DoS) attack was modeled using Stochastic Well-formed Nets (SWNs). The researchers investigated how these two models can be integrated to characterize the DoS attack impact. While the approach is focused on specific scenarios, the executed analysis illustrated that the user satisfaction of a power line can differ significantly depending on the severity and progression of the DoS attack.

In a different work, Bloomfield et al. [10] centered their study on how the strength of dependencies between power and telecommunication networks affects various measures of risk and uncertainty. The approach begins with a high level of abstraction aiming to identify dependencies between the components of CIs, which is then followed by a detailed service behavior model. Furthermore, the authors employed probabilistic models to come up with various measures for risk assessment, e.g., the likelihood of cascade failure under a given set of assumptions.

Netkachov et al. [43] used stochastic modeling of an industrial control system and studied the effect of both accidental failure and cyber-attacks. In fact, the researchers used a stochastic state machine to model the behavior of the adversary, while the dependencies between the elements are modeled using a deterministic or a probabilistic approach. The study of the employed approach unveiled the most critical elements of the network and a high correlation between the impact and the capability of the attackers.

Furthermore, Johansen et al. [26] proposed to model the interdependencies by using a Bayesian network and a minimum link set (MLS) formulation to create the network model. The latter represented a set of functioning components required from the system to function. Moreover, the authors distinguished three types of dependencies: service provision, geographic, and access to repair interdependencies. This dependency relationship was then defined by the joint probability distribution of the components. Regardless of parent choice, the entire system is defined using joint probabilities divided by the marginal chances of failure. By applying their framework on a real system and given the complex interdependencies, the researchers quantified the cascading effect of an individual component's performance on the entire network performance.

Additionally, Heracleous et al. [24] proposed a dependency modeling method that supports the investigation of the cascading effect, performs vulnerability analysis, and plans maintenance strategies. The authors demonstrated how an open hybrid automata allows modeling individual subsystems and composing them together to create more complex and detailed systems with the aim to capture different types of dependencies. By connecting six open automata models that represent various components of CIs, the authors ran simulations to study the effect of the malfunctioning of one infrastructure on other elements, perform vulnerability analysis, and offer a maintenance plan.

In another work, Ferdowsi et al. [20] analyzed the problem of allocating security resources over the various components of interdependent cyber-physical systems (CPSs) in order to protect the entire ecosystem against cyber-attacks. Indeed, the authors formulated a Colonel Blotto game where the attacker seeks to allocate its resources with the intention of compromising the CPS. At the same time, the defender chooses how to prioritize the defense against potential attacks. The reported result illustrated the correlation between the attacker's knowledge of interdependencies and the defense's success.

To compare dependency models, the following criteria are considered: categories of dependencies, completeness, and modeling approach.

- *Categories of dependencies:* this criterion refers to the types of interdependencies that each method models. In this context, we classify these as cyber, physical, and functional dependencies [49]. Additionally, we label the modeled dependencies as cyber if the state of one domain depends on information transmitted by another. Moreover, physical dependencies represent the networks that share a physical flow. Furthermore, functional dependencies consider, in (or the availability of) one domain, the effect of degradation on the performance of the dependent infrastructure.
- *Scale:* this criterion measures the coverage of the reviewed methods. Clearly, the number of considered dependent domains directly affects the completeness of the modeled architecture.
- *Modeling approach:* this criterion labels the method based on the technique employed to model dependencies: probabilistic (P), expert opinion (E), or deterministic (D).

Table 3.5 summarizes the characteristics above and compares the surveyed methods by producing the following observations. First, all the approaches concentrate on the downstream dependencies and maintain a high level of detail where each domain is represented as one entity. Indeed, this might indicate that cyber dependencies require an additional modeling approach in order to analyze the effect

Table 3.5 Comparison of the methods modeling dependencies between smart cities' elements. (Modeling approaches: P—probabilistic, E—expert opinion, D—deterministic.)

Reference	Category			Scale			Modeling approach		
	Cyber	Physical	Functional	<3	3–5	>5	P	E	D
Laugé et al. [32]			✓			✓		✓	
König et al. [30]			✓	✓			✓		
Stergiopoulos et al. [55]			✓	✓				✓	
Stergiopoulos et al. [56]			✓			✓		✓	
Beccuti et al. [9]			✓	✓			✓		
Bloomfield et al. [10]		✓	✓	✓			✓		✓
Netkachov et al. [43]	✓			✓			✓		✓
Johansen et al. [26]	✓	✓			✓		✓		
Heracleous et al. [24]					✓				
Ferdowsi et al. [20]	✓	✓		✓			✓		

of cyber-attacks targeting the data layer. Second, the surveyed methods support a limited number of domains, which implies that these methods are developed as a proof of concept and that the feasibility of a practical implementation requires further investigation. In fact, the scalability of the method and its accuracy should be carefully considered, even though the accuracy evaluation measures remain.

3.2 Analytics-Driven Cyber Situational Awareness for Smart City: Are We There Yet?

3.2.1 Toward Threat Coverage

Table 3.6 shows a connection between threat classes (Chap. 2, Sect. 2.3.3) and the corresponding cyber situational awareness methods. Notably, threats related to infrastructure and data received the most attention, while discovery threats, including user credentials, are rarely researched. Similarly, threats such as data tampering and data misuse are also insufficiently studied. Given the worldwide growth of ransomware attacks against smart cities, the latter is surprising. The reviewed works cover one threat category with rare exceptions, leaving other threats unaddressed. Furthermore, their limited scope might impede the transition to practical applications.

3.2.2 Toward Human Cognition Engagement

Just as significant, analytics-driven cybersecurity needs to offer visual support in order to engage human cognition for data interpretation. Visual analytics connect computational data analysis methods and human reasoning in the decision-making process through visualization and interaction. Indeed, the graphical representation conveys a broad spectrum of visual aids to understand how the model works, to represent the results in an intuitive, self-explanatory way, and to enable interaction for visual data exploration. While the reviewed works have not been dedicated to producing a visual aid, we compare visual dimensions to understand the role of visualization for analytical analysis. To this end, one can derive (and focus) on three categories, namely, performance visualization, model explanation, and knowledge extraction.

- *Performance visualization* refers to the graphical representation of the model's accuracy, including the one achieved by employing different parameters in the model.
- *Model explanation* refers to the process of interpreting the discovered knowledge in the form of visual graphics. The first thing to consider here is the visualization of model architecture, in particular, how the model and dataflow are designed.

Table 3.6 A connection between threat classes and perception methods

Threat category	Level 1: Perception	Level 2: Comprehension	Level 3: Projection
Identity theft		[15]	
Resource discovery		[11, 15]	
Infrastructure tampering	[29, 36, 46]	[11, 15, 27]	
Resource overwhelming	[34, 48, 53]	[52, 54]	[9, 10]
Identity manipulation	[48, 53]	[19, 54]	
Malware spreading	[6, 14]	[15]	
Input manipulation			
Data tampering	[7]		
Data corruption	[23, 45, 48]	[23, 35, 54]	
Data misuse		[57]	
Decision-making process disruption	[8]		
Overall threat factor/impact		[4, 28, 38, 39, 52, 58]	[9, 10, 26, 30, 32, 43, 55, 56]

Table 3.7 The distribution of visualization types. The papers that consider two different visualization categories are illustrated close to the line that distinguishes two categories

Visualization category	Level 1: Perception	Level 2: Comprehension	Level 3: Projection
Performance visualization	[6–8, 14, 23, 31, 46]	[38, 58]	[55]
Model explanation	[6–8, 29, 31, 33, 36, 48, 53]	[11, 18, 28, 38, 52, 54, 58]	[10, 24, 26, 30]
Knowledge extraction	[45, 46, 48, 53]	[4, 11, 27, 35, 39, 52, 57]	[9, 10, 20, 24, 26, 32, 56]

Additionally, computational graphs and flowcharts sufficiently capture the architecture. Moreover, other components to visualize are the model parameters, the contribution of different inputs (i.e., features), and the error measurements (e.g., those generated by adversarial network samples at each step).

- *Knowledge extraction* leverages human cognition which enables users to interpret data and formulate hypotheses more efficiently. In fact, interaction techniques, such as detail-on-demand, dynamic queries, and zooming, can significantly improve this process.

Table 3.7 illustrates the distribution of the types of the offered visualizations. Even though around 50% of the works still do not leverage a visualization method, the researchers found a way to visually clarify a model as a means to explain a method. Indeed, scatterplots and line and bar charts are gradually used as visual structure for model explanation. In fact, the majority of reviewed works used spatial view in the form of two-dimensional data representation, while the combination of a physical and two-dimensional structure is only used in one paper. Furthermore, less than 40% of the surveyed models support result visualization. Among them, only one work offers interactivity, while the remaining works solely rely on non-interactive representations.

Although automated algorithms make pattern recognition, classification, and other functions possible, the combination of these algorithms with visual analytics can undoubtedly enhance the decision-making process.

3.2.3 Toward Data Availability

The reviewed works established a basis for researchers by obtaining underlying data in two ways: (i) using existing datasets and (ii) harvesting data by setting up specific environments in laboratory settings. The former methods are quite efficient given that they avoid any data collection. However, we witness a shortage of smart cities-related datasets. Therefore, the second method of data capture is highly thought-after. Nevertheless, it is typically only suitable for short-term collection, hardly reproducible, and barely covers the entire infrastructure of smart cities.

Tables 3.8, 3.9, 3.10 provide a summary of data inputs, the output (interpretation) of the model, and the used datasets for validation.

Given the lack of public datasets that are created for smart cities, the general examples and several datasets are produced in laboratory environments. However, such settings do not capture a smart cities' context. Therefore, they are rarely based on realistic assumptions; thus, their practical implementation might not always be successful or representative. We now give a brief description of the employed public datasets.

2016 SWaT dataset [21] supports research in the design of secure Cyber-Physical Systems (CPSs). Indeed, the data collection was performed on a six-stage Secure Water Treatment (SWaT) testbed that depicts a scaled-down version of an industrial water treatment plant. Additionally, the dataset consists of two behavioral models collected during normal operation and an under attack system.

Moreover, the physical properties of the data along with the network traffic contain attacks carried out by the researchers and provide accurate data labels for subsequent use. Shodan [1] is a search engine for Internet-connected devices. It crawls the Internet 24/7 and updates its repository in real time to provide a recent list of IoT devices. Additionally, by grabbing and analyzing banners and device meta-data, the engine explores their corresponding various vulnerabilities (including Heartbleed, Logjam, and default passwords).

BullGuard's IoT Scanner is an online search engine that leverages Shodan's service in order to allow users to scan their networks for vulnerabilities.

A darknet [2] (also commonly referred to as a network telescope) is a set of routable and allocated yet unused IP addresses. From a design perspective, a darknet is transparent and indistinguishable compared with the rest of the Internet space. From a deployment perspective, it is rendered by network sensors that are implemented and dispersed on numerous strategic points throughout the Internet. The aim of a darknet is to provide a lens on Internet-wide unsolicited traffic; since darknet IP addresses are unused, any traffic targeting them represents anomalous traffic.

All ransomware and malware samples are collected from VirusTotal. Indeed, this service combines the output from various antivirus programs and online scan engines to test whether the behavior of the software indicates malicious activities or not. Additionally, through the public API, the users can automatically upload and verify their files.

3.3 Summary

The analytics-driven cyber situational awareness for smart cities attracts researchers in many ways, from detecting attacks to assessing risks and modeling dependencies. Understanding what has already been tried provides lessons learned and enables further advancement. Three significant findings emerged from the literature review.

Table 3.8 Summary of base data and datasets. Level 1: Perception

Reference	Base data																					Interpretation	Dataset
	System components	Type of components	Physical topology	Functional relations	Stochastic assoc.	List of IoT devices	List of vulnerabilities	Probability of attack	Attack tree	Countermeasures	Real-world attack	Impact model	Sensor readings	Actuator state	Load profile	Power usage	OpCode	RPL DODAG	ETX	Network activity	NS traffic		
Oza et al. [45]													✓									Data integrity violation	Lab simulation
He et al. [23]															✓							Data integrity violation	Live power test system
Azmoodeh et al. [6]																	✓					Malware detection	Live IoT apps. Malware samples
Dovom et al. [14]																	✓					Malware detection	Live apps. Ransomware samples
Kumar et al. [29]																				✓		Detected anomaly	Lab setup (live network traffic)
Shreenivas et al. [53]																		✓	✓			Detected malicious node	Lab simulation
Li et al. [34]													✓	✓								Detected anomaly	2016 SWaT dataset
Azmoodeh et al. [7]																✓						Ransomware detection	Live apps. Ransomware samples
Baracaldo et al. [8]													✓									Integrity violation	Artificial dataset
Laishram & Phoha [31]													✓									Integrity violation	MNIST

Table 3.9 Summary of base data and datasets. Level 2: Comprehension

Reference	Base data																					Interpretation	Dataset
	System components	Type of components	Physical topology	Functional relations	Stochastic assoc.	List of IoT devices	List of vulnerabilities	Probability of attack	Attack tree	Countermeasures	Real-world attack	Impact model	Sensor readings	Actuator state	Load profile	Power usage	OpCode	RPL DODAG	ETX	Network activity	NS traffic		
Li et al. [35]	✓						✓		✓	✓												Priority for mitigation	Lab simulation
Kelarestaghi et al. [27]											✓	✓										Impact assessment	Collection of publications
Kotzanikolaou et al. [28]	✓		✓									✓										Priority for mitigation	Lab simulation
Sicari at al. [54]							✓		✓	✓												Exploitability level	General example
Wang et al. [57]							✓		✓	✓												Ranked vulnerabilities	Lab simulation
Radanliev et al. [47]						✓																Economic impact	BullGuard's IoT Scanner
Mohammad [38]	✓	✓					✓	✓	✓													Risk level	General example
Shivraj et al. [52]	✓						✓	✓	✓													Risk level	Lab simulation
Mohsin et al. [39]	✓	✓					✓	✓	✓													Risk level	General example
Falco et al. [19]									✓													Attack plan	General example
Angelini et al. [4]	✓								✓			✓										Impact on the process mission	Live power distribution system
Wang et al. [58]	✓	✓																				Contextualized threat intelligence	General example
Bou-Harb et al. [11]						✓															✓	Contextualized threat intelligence	Darknet; Shodan
Dowling et al. [15]																				✓	✓	Attack vectors and patterns	Honeypot

Table 3.10 Summary of base data and datasets. Level 3: Projection

Reference	Base data																					Interpretation	Dataset
	System components	Type of components	Physical topology	Functional relations	Stochastic assoc.	List of IoT devices	List of vulnerabilities	Probability of attack	Attack tree	Countermeasures	Real-world attack	Impact model	Sensor readings	Actuator state	Load profile	Power usage	OpCode	RPL DODAG	ETX	Network activity	NS traffic		
Laugé et al. [32]	✓											✓										Level of interdep.	Expert opinion
König et al. [30]	✓	✓																				Level of interdep.	Lab simulation
Stergiopoulos et al. [55]	✓		✓																			Priority for mitigation	Lab simulation
Stergiopoulos et al. [56]	✓		✓																			Evolution of dependencies	Lab setup
Beccuti et al. [9]				✓	✓																	Level of interdependencies	Testbed
Bloomfield et al. [10]			✓	✓	✓																	Impact of coupled subsystem	Live infrastructure
Netkachov et al. [43]	✓				✓																	Impact on the system under study	A power transmission network
Johansen et al. [26]	✓		✓																			Level of interdependencies	A network of interdependent systems
Ferdowsi et al. [20]	✓		✓																			Priority for mitigation	Generic example

First, cyber situational awareness in the context of smart cities seems to be in a juvenile stage. Indeed, cyber dependencies between the various components of smart cities' infrastructure are not thoroughly studied. However, the research should put identified threats and ongoing attacks in the context of smart cities' operations. It should consider interdependencies among domains to realize a real impact on mission-critical services. Additionally, more interdisciplinary research is required to capture the dependencies between different components of the smart cities ecosystem, including cyber-related ones. Moreover, researchers should investigate cyber dependencies, safety, financial, and operational effects to realize the impact of cyber-attacks on different components. Furthermore, from the visual perspective, the result of the investigation might need effective representation to capture such cyber dependencies.

Second, cyber-related data for smart cities are increasingly unavailable. Establishing relevant datasets with a broad scope and sufficient raw data can solve the evaluation problem and improve the threat landscape's visibility.

Third, in the context of smart cities, research should give more attention to evaluating the reviewed methods' credibility and transparency. Indeed, by doing so, we could transition from these methods to more practical implementation. However, the reliability metrics of threat prioritization techniques are not well established yet. Additionally, it is practically impossible to establish a ground truth due to many reasons:

- The visibility of interdomain dependencies in the entire ecosystem is limited.
- Accessing past cybersecurity incidents is hard.
- Empirical data for comparison is minimal.

For the visual analytics community, it could symbolize the creation of visual techniques to reveal the insights of machine learning models or to create a visual representation of threats progression through the entire system of smart cities.

References

1. Shodan®. http://shodan.io. Accessed: 2020-03-15.
2. UCSD Network Telescope – Near-Real-Time Network Telescope Dataset. http://www.caida.org/data/passive/telescope-near-real-time_dataset.xml. Accessed: 2020-03-05.
3. Saad Albawi, Tareq Abed Mohammed, and Saad Al-Zawi. Understanding of a convolutional neural network. In *2017 International Conference on Engineering and Technology (ICET)*, pages 1–6. Ieee, 2017.
4. Marco Angelini and Giuseppe Santucci. Visual cyber situational awareness for critical infrastructures. In *Proceedings of the 8th International Symposium on Visual Information Communication and Interaction*, pages 83–92, 2015.
5. Terje Aven and Bjørnar Heide. Reliability and validity of risk analysis. *Reliability Engineering & System Safety*, 94(11):1862–1868, 2009.
6. Amin Azmoodeh, Ali Dehghantanha, and Kim-Kwang Raymond Choo. Robust malware detection for internet of (battlefield) things devices using deep eigenspace learning. *IEEE Transactions on Sustainable Computing*, 4(1):88–95, 2018.

7. Amin Azmoodeh, Ali Dehghantanha, Mauro Conti, and Kim-Kwang Raymond Choo. Detecting crypto-ransomware in IoT networks based on energy consumption footprint. *Journal of Ambient Intelligence and Humanized Computing*, 9(4):1141–1152, 2018.
8. N. Baracaldo, B. Chen, H. Ludwig, A. Safavi, and R. Zhang. Detecting Poisoning Attacks on Machine Learning in IoT Environments. In *2018 IEEE International Congress on Internet of Things (ICIOT)*, pages 57–64, 2018.
9. Marco Beccuti, Silvano Chiaradonna, Felicita Di Giandomenico, Susanna Donatelli, Giovanna Dondossola, and Giuliana Franceschinis. Quantification of dependencies between electrical and information infrastructures. *International Journal of Critical Infrastructure Protection*, 5(1):14–27, 2012.
10. Robin E Bloomfield, Peter Popov, Kizito Salako, Vladimir Stankovic, and David Wright. Preliminary interdependency analysis: An approach to support critical-infrastructure risk-assessment. *Reliability Engineering & System Safety*, 167:198–217, 2017.
11. Elias Bou-Harb and Nataliia Neshenko. *Cyber Threat Intelligence for the Internet of Things*. Springer, 2020.
12. Giovanni Chiola, Claude Dutheillet, Giuliana Franceschinis, and Serge Haddad. Stochastic well-formed colored nets and symmetric modeling applications. *IEEE Transactions on Computers*, 42(11):1343–1360, 1993.
13. Herbert Aron David and Melvin L Moeschberger. *The Theory of Competing Risks: HA David, ML Moeschberger*. C. Griffin, 1978.
14. Ensieh Modiri Dovom, Amin Azmoodeh, Ali Dehghantanha, David Ellis Newton, Reza M Parizi, and Hadis Karimipour. Fuzzy pattern tree for edge malware detection and categorization in IoT. *Journal of Systems Architecture*, 97:1–7, 2019.
15. Seamus Dowling, Michael Schukat, and Hugh Melvin. A ZigBee honeypot to assess IoT cyberattack behaviour. In *2017 28th Irish Signals and Systems Conference (ISSC)*, pages 1–6. IEEE, 2017.
16. Stefan Edelkamp and Stefan Schrödl. Chapter 1 - Introduction. In Stefan Edelkamp and Stefan Schrödl, editors, *Heuristic Search*, pages 3 – 46. Morgan Kaufmann, San Francisco, 2012.
17. Mica R Endsley. Toward a theory of situation awareness in dynamic systems. *Human factors*, 37(1):32–64, 1995.
18. Gregory Falco, Carlos Caldera, and Howard Shrobe. IIOT cybersecurity risk modeling for Scada systems. *IEEE Internet of Things Journal*, 5(6):4486–4495, 2018.
19. Gregory Falco, Arun Viswanathan, Carlos Caldera, and Howard Shrobe. A master attack methodology for an ai-based automated attack planner for smart cities. *IEEE Access*, 6:48360–48373, 2018.
20. Aidin Ferdowsi, Walid Saad, Behrouz Maham, and Narayan B Mandayam. A Colonel Blotto game for interdependence-aware cyber-physical systems security in smart cities. In *Proceedings of the 2nd International Workshop on Science of Smart City Operations and Platforms Engineering*, pages 7–12, 2017.
21. Jonathan Goh, Sridhar Adepu, Khurum Nazir Junejo, and Aditya Mathur. A dataset to support research in the design of secure water treatment systems. In *International Conference on Critical Information Infrastructures Security*, pages 88–99. Springer, 2016.
22. Ian Goodfellow, Yoshua Bengio, and Aaron Courville. *Deep Learning*. MIT Press, 2016.
23. Youbiao He, Gihan J Mendis, and Jin Wei. Real-time detection of false data injection attacks in smart grid: A deep learning-based intelligent mechanism. *IEEE Transactions on Smart Grid*, 8(5):2505–2516, 2017. Publisher: IEEE.
24. Constantinos Heracleous, Panayiotis Kolios, Christos G Panayiotou, Georgios Ellinas, and Marios M Polycarpou. Hybrid systems modeling for critical infrastructures interdependency analysis. *Reliability Engineering & System Safety*, 165:89–101, 2017.
25. Geoffrey E Hinton, Simon Osindero, and Yee-Whye Teh. *A fast learning algorithm for deep belief nets*, volume 18. MIT Press One Rogers Street, Cambridge, MA 02142-1209, USA journals-info . . . , 2006.

26. Chloe Johansen and Iris Tien. Probabilistic multi-scale modeling of interdependencies between critical infrastructure systems for resilience. *Sustainable and Resilient Infrastructure*, 3(1):1–15, 2018.
27. Kaveh Bakhsh Kelarestaghi, Mahsa Foruhandeh, Kevin Heaslip, and Ryan Gerdes. Intelligent transportation system security: impact-oriented risk assessment of in-vehicle networks. *IEEE Intelligent Transportation Systems Magazine, doi*, 10, 2019.
28. Panayiotis Kotzanikolaou, Marianthi Theoharidou, and Dimitris Gritzalis. Assessing n-order dependencies between critical infrastructures. *International Journal of Critical Infrastructures 6*, 9(1):93–110, 2013.
29. A. Kumar and T. J. Lim. EDIMA: Early Detection of IoT Malware Network Activity Using Machine Learning Techniques. In *2019 IEEE 5th World Forum on Internet of Things (WF-IoT)*, pages 289–294, April 2019.
30. Sandra König and Stefan Rass. Investigating stochastic dependencies between critical infrastructures. *Int. J. Adv. Syst. Meas*, 11:250–258, 2018.
31. Ricky Laishram and Vir Virander Phoha. Curie: A method for protecting SVM Classifier from Poisoning Attack. *arXiv preprint arXiv:1606.01584*, 2016.
32. Ana Laugé, Josune Hernantes, and Jose M Sarriegi. Critical infrastructure dependencies: A holistic, dynamic and quantitative approach. *International Journal of Critical Infrastructure Protection*, 8:16–23, 2015.
33. Dan Li, Dacheng Chen, Jonathan Goh, and See-kiong Ng. Anomaly Detection with Generative Adversarial Networks for Multivariate Time Series. *arXiv preprint arXiv:1809.04758*, 2018.
34. Dan Li, Dacheng Chen, Baihong Jin, Lei Shi, Jonathan Goh, and See-Kiong Ng. MAD-GAN: Multivariate anomaly detection for time series data with generative adversarial networks. In *International Conference on Artificial Neural Networks*, pages 703–716. Springer, 2019.
35. Zhiyi Li, Dong Jin, Christopher Hannon, Mohammad Shahidehpour, and Jianhui Wang. Assessing and mitigating cybersecurity risks of traffic light systems in smart cities. *IET Cyber-Physical Systems: Theory & Applications*, 1(1):60–69, 2016.
36. Yair Meidan, Michael Bohadana, Yael Mathov, Yisroel Mirsky, Asaf Shabtai, Dominik Breitenbacher, and Yuval Elovici. N-BaIoT –network-based detection of IoT botnet attacks using deep autoencoders. *IEEE Pervasive Computing*, 17(3):12–22, 2018.
37. Peter Mell, Karen Scarfone, and Sasha Romanosky. Common vulnerability scoring system. *IEEE Security & Privacy*, 4(6):85–89, 2006.
38. Nazeeruddin Mohammad. A Multi-Tiered Defense Model for the Security Analysis of Critical Facilities in Smart Cities. *IEEE Access*, 7:152585–152598, 2019.
39. Mujahid Mohsin, Muhammad Usama Sardar, Osman Hasan, and Zahid Anwar. IoTRiskAnalyzer: a probabilistic model checking based framework for formal risk analytics of the Internet of Things. *IEEE Access*, 5:5494–5505, 2017.
40. D. R. Naik, L. B. Das, and T. S. Bindiya. Wireless Sensor networks with Zigbee and WiFi for Environment Monitoring, Traffic Management and Vehicle Monitoring in Smart Cities. In *2018 IEEE 3rd International Conference on Computing, Communication and Security (ICCCS)*, pages 46–50, 2018.
41. Nataliia Neshenko, Elias Bou-Harb, Jorge Crichigno, Georges Kaddoum, and Nasir Ghani. Demystifying IoT security: an exhaustive survey on IoT vulnerabilities and a first empirical look on internet-scale IoT exploitations. *IEEE Communications Surveys & Tutorials*, 21(3):2702–2733, 2019.
42. Nataliia Neshenko, Christelle Nader, Elias Bou-Harb, and Borko Furht. A survey of methods supporting cyber situational awareness in the context of smart cities. *Journal of Big Data*, 7(1):1–41, 2020. Publisher: SpringerOpen.
43. Oleksandr Netkachov, Peter Popov, and Kizito Salako. Quantification of the impact of cyber attack in critical infrastructures. In *International Conference on Computer Safety, Reliability, and Security*, pages 316–327. Springer, 2014.
44. J. R. C. Nurse, S. Creese, and D. De Roure. Security Risk Assessment in Internet of Things Systems. *IT Professional*, 19(5):20–26, 2017.

45. Pratham Oza, Mahsa Foruhandeh, Ryan Gerdes, and Thidapat Chantem. Secure Traffic Lights: Replay Attack Detection for Model-based Smart Traffic Controllers. In *Proceedings of the Second ACM Workshop on Automotive and Aerial Vehicle Security*, pages 5–10, 2020.
46. V. R, M. Alazab, S. Srinivasan, Q. Pham, S. Kotti Padannayil, and K. Simran. A Visualized Botnet Detection System based Deep Learning for the Internet of Things Networks of Smart Cities. *IEEE Transactions on Industry Applications*, pages 1–1, 2020.
47. Petar Radanliev, David Charles De Roure, Razvan Nicolescu, Michael Huth, Rafael Mantilla Montalvo, Stacy Cannady, and Peter Burnap. Future developments in cyber risk assessment for the internet of things. *Computers in Industry*, 102:14–22, 2018.
48. Shahid Raza, Linus Wallgren, and Thiemo Voigt. SVELTE: Real-time intrusion detection in the Internet of Things. *Ad hoc networks*, 11(8):2661–2674, 2013.
49. Steven M Rinaldi, James P Peerenboom, and Terrence K Kelly. Identifying, understanding, and analyzing critical infrastructure interdependencies. *IEEE control systems magazine*, 21(6):11–25, 2001.
50. R. Senge and E. Hüllermeier. Fast Fuzzy Pattern Tree Learning for Classification. *IEEE Transactions on Fuzzy Systems*, 23(6):2024–2033, 2015.
51. Alireza Shameli-Sendi, Rouzbeh Aghababaei-Barzegar, and Mohamed Cheriet. Taxonomy of information security risk assessment (ISRA). *Computers & security*, 57:14–30, 2016.
52. VL Shivraj, MA Rajan, and P Balamuralidhar. A graph theory based generic risk assessment framework for internet of things (IoT). In *2017 IEEE International Conference on Advanced Networks and Telecommunications Systems (ANTS)*, pages 1–6. IEEE, 2017.
53. Dharmini Shreenivas, Shahid Raza, and Thiemo Voigt. Intrusion detection in the RPL-connected 6LoWPAN networks. In *Proceedings of the 3rd ACM international workshop on IoT privacy, trust, and security*, pages 31–38, 2017.
54. Sabrina Sicari, Alessandra Rizzardi, Daniele Miorandi, and Alberto Coen-Porisini. A risk assessment methodology for the Internet of Things. *Computer Communications*, 129:67–79, 2018.
55. George Stergiopoulos, Panayiotis Kotzanikolaou, Marianthi Theocharidou, and Dimitris Gritzalis. Risk mitigation strategies for critical infrastructures based on graph centrality analysis. *International Journal of Critical Infrastructure Protection*, 10:34–44, 2015.
56. George Stergiopoulos, Panayiotis Kotzanikolaou, Marianthi Theocharidou, Georgia Lykou, and Dimitris Gritzalis. Time-based critical infrastructure dependency analysis for large-scale and cross-sectoral failures. *International Journal of Critical Infrastructure Protection*, 12:46–60, 2016.
57. Huan Wang, Zhanfang Chen, Jianping Zhao, Xiaoqiang Di, and Dan Liu. A vulnerability assessment method in industrial internet of things based on attack graph and maximum flow. *Ieee Access*, 6:8599–8609, 2018.
58. P. Wang, A. Ali, and W. Kelly. Data security and threat modeling for smart city infrastructure. In *2015 International Conference on Cyber Security of Smart Cities, Industrial Control System and Communications (SSIC)*, pages 1–6, August 2015.
59. Shuangbao Paul Wang and Robert S Ledley. *Computer architecture and security: Fundamentals of designing secure computer systems*. John Wiley & Sons, 2012.
60. Yang Xin, Lingshuang Kong, Zhi Liu, Yuling Chen, Yanmiao Li, Hongliang Zhu, Mingcheng Gao, Haixia Hou, and Chunhua Wang. Machine learning and deep learning methods for cybersecurity. *IEEE Access*, 6:35365–35381, 2018.

Chapter 4
Cyber Situational Awareness for Industrial Control Systems (ICSs) Deployed in Smart City

The increased number of cyber-attacks against critical infrastructure, in particular, their vulnerable network-assessable automated control systems, paved the way for new approaches to defining cyber situational awareness for smart cities. This chapter defines the activities required to enforce a sound situational awareness program and elaborates on design challenges that hinder the transition to operation in ICS realms. In this context, cybersecurity operators and investigators work with a massive amount of logs collected by a large number of heterogeneous ICS assets. The detection and prompt analysis of cyber-attacks in smart city realms is a complex task that can rarely be solved using only automatic methods. It is vital to integrate cognitive and computational approaches to efficiently identify the most scathing attacks for their targeted remediation and forensics. To this end, this chapter introduces a framework to enhance situational awareness by providing evidence-based insights about ongoing cyber incidents and respective system responses to assist decision-making.

In Sect. 4.1, this chapter briefly describes the situational awareness process and its elements. Section 4.2 introduces the overview and details the design components of the situational awareness framework that can be integrated into the operation in the ICS realm to support the prompt decision-making process. The feedback mechanism (in the form of an evaluation strategy) to enhance the process and the underlying technology is presented in Sect. 4.3. Finally, Sect. 4.4 concludes the chapter.

4.1 Development of Successful Situational Awareness Program

Situational awareness is a supportive process to ensure that cybersecurity operators and decision-makers possess all required information to be able to take appropriate

Fig. 4.1 Situational
awareness process

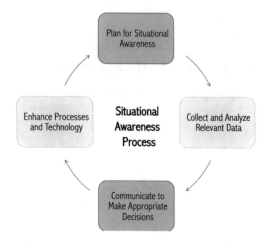

steps to prepare incident and controls management processes, vulnerability, service continuity, and risk management strategies.

The four-phase situational awareness process [10] is illustrated in Fig. 4.1. It incorporates the activities to plan for, conduct, communicate, and enhance situational awareness to meet operational cyber resilience requirements.

The four phases of this process are briefly outlined below to highlight the corresponding details of the framework introduced in this chapter.

4.1.1 Plan for Situational Awareness

The first step in the successful execution of a situational awareness program is planning, which is a formal process that describes the goals, required steps to achieve these goals, and the resources to execute the plan. Particularly, the plan should consist of the definition of the strategy, data collection methodologies, and analytical result communication plan.

4.1.2 Collect and Analyze Relevant Data

To achieve planned goals, the situation awareness process should include the identification of the required data to support the required detection, resilience, and impact measures. It is vital to consider the vantage point of various users of information and their particular needs. For instance, the decision-makers might need consolidated information that includes critical metrics to make prompt decisions, while cybersecurity analysts require to investigate data from top-level metrics to the raw data.

In the beginning, required measures should be established to provide important information on what data to collect and how periodically to do so. Furthermore, the formal procedures provide detailed step-by-step guidance on the data collection process, including details related to data format. The next step is a selection of the data analysis approach and the methods of extracting valuable insights. One important aspect that should not be overlooked is the establishment of the infrastructure for continuous improvement of situational awareness programs. The final step is the implementation of the pipeline for real-time collection, data storage, and analysis.

4.1.3   Communicate to Make Appropriate Decisions

A fundamental provision of situational awareness is appropriate communication and information exchange [38]. As mentioned, the communication has to be tailored to the needs of a particular group of users.

Communication can take many forms, for instance, text messages, alerts, automatic notifications, comprehensive reports, and alike. A notable form of communication and information exchange is its visualization. Visual analytics permits the structure of complex data, recognition of patterns, and acquaintance with how individual elements are connected. In this context, various visualization tools and techniques such as knowledge maps, color codes, charts, attention icons, and dynamic interaction can be useful.

The following critical elements should be covered and properly defined to establish proper communication and deliver sound situational awareness to support a prompt decision-making process.

- Identify stakeholders and their informational needs
- Identify what critical information will be communicated
- Define communication standards
- Establish dissemination channels (email, mobile notifications, etc.)
- Define appropriate procedure and timeline for data retention
- Identify who will be responsible for data sharing
- Set up appropriate infrastructure

For the complex environment, more frequent communication might be required to maintain appropriate situational awareness. However, the most important point here is the quality, not the quantity, of the shared information.

4.1.4   Enhance Process and Technology

Successful protection from cyber threats and risk mitigation heavily depends on the effectiveness of the situational awareness program [10]. Given that cyber threats against smart cities continuously evolve, it is critical to maintain the effectiveness of established procedures, including those that support situational awareness. Periodical review, identification of potential improvements, and delivery of essential modifications are the main activities herein.

Inspired by the approach above, the following section introduces the framework for evidence-based insights regarding the timeline and respective system responses during the cyber incident to assist decision-making in ICS settings.

4.2   Framework Overview

Sound cyber situational awareness requirements aim to help cyber operators to focus their efforts on the correct assets, useful data, and usage of appropriate techniques to convert data into valuable analytics. This section overviews and details core components of the proposed framework aiming to support situational awareness in the context of ICS deployed in the critical infrastructure of smart cities.

4.2.1   Design Considerations

Numerous research and operating efforts are dedicated to the development of various methods to support situational awareness for ICS assets. Existing methods in this area include control-theoretic approaches, various machine learning algorithms, and visual analytics.

The underlying assumption behind the control-theoretical approaches is the presence of the mathematical model for a particular ICS and its process. The approach converts a physical process of ICS to a mathematical instance. It then uses the model to monitor system operation, detect deviations from expected behavior, and investigate cyber incidents. Some notable works representing this approach include the following. Pasqualetti et al. [34] employed system- and graph-theoretic techniques to identify and characterize the vulnerabilities of a network of the power grid. The authors used Luenberger-type detection filters as a fundamental method for cyber-attack detection. Along the same line, Mo et al. [32] focused on attack scenarios in which the adversary registers regular system measurements to produce statistically identical yet malicious data for further injection into the system. To detect this type of malicious activity, the authors leveraged physical watermarking to authenticate the correct operation of the system. The injection of a known noisy input into a physical system, leading to controllable physical properties changes, was used to detect the attack. Chabukswar et al. [9] extended noisy control to multi-input, multi-output systems of chemical plants and microgrids.

Alternatively, Bou-Harb et al. [6] modeled a semantic behavioral graph consisting of malicious attack signatures, which are retrieved from active cyber threat intelligence, and data flows extracted from the physical layer. Substantial similarities between semantic graphs represented indicators of ongoing malicious activities. Furthermore, Khanna et al. [21] operated a control-theoretic Hidden Markov Model (HMM) for intrusion detection in ad hoc wireless networks. An observed deviation from predetermined rules that govern the system's behavior holds an elevated likelihood of ongoing attack.

Consideration 1: Obtaining and maintaining a process model is the most challenging task for control-theoretic approaches. For instance, ICS can have an incompatible structure, depending on their type and used technology. Moreover, continuous modification and process optimization challenge the preservation of such models. Therefore, employing the identical model-based attack detection technique for ICS deployed in different industries seems to be unrealistic.

Therefore, operating and research communities explore methods that are scalable and can be directly employed for different systems. For instance, researchers consider data-driven methods, including those that leverage machine learning to address the major challenge of the control-theoretic approaches.

Consideration 2: The rarity of attack-related empirical data challenges the adoption of supervised methods for attack detection in ICS.

To this end, several research works employed various unsupervised machine learning methods for the inference of anomalies in the behavior of ICS deployed in critical infrastructure. For attack detection, unsupervised methods consider multivariate or single time series. The majority of these approaches formulate attack detection as an anomaly detection problem. Indeed, significant deviation from the expected system behavior might indicate an ongoing cyber-attack or system failure that endanger core cybersecurity requirements of availability, integrity, and confidentiality.

Inoue et al. [19] considered Deep Neural Network (DNN) and one class Support Vector Machine (OSVM) as an attack detection mechanism. The SVM classifier demonstrated a better attack detection rate though it led to a higher false alarm rate than those derived using the DNN-based approach. In an alternative work, Elnour et al. [13] suggested the use of a semi-supervised method rooted in the Dual Isolation Forest (DIF) model for the same purpose. The approach is comprised of two independently trained isolation forest models. The first was trained using the normalized raw data, while another operated pre-processed version of the data using Principal Component Analysis (PCA). Furthermore, Li et al. [25] put forward an unsupervised GAN-based anomaly detection method and modeled nonlinear correlation among multiple time series. The method employed Long Short-Term Recurrent Neural Networks (LSTM-RNNs) for underlying neural networks and calculated scores to indicate the level of abnormality in the time series. Lin et al. [26] combined time automata learning and Bayesian neural network to infer the abnormal behavior of ICS assets, rendering inference of a wide range of attacks.

Consideration 3: To sustain the objective of prioritization in situation awareness process, the method of cyber incident detection should reveal a specific asset that is connected to anomalies [33].

To this end, researchers examine two alternative strategies: model-agnostic and model-specific frameworks for anomaly localization.

One of the model-agnostic method was suggested and widely used generic framework, dubbed as LIME, that explains the prediction of any classifier [36]. The technique recognized a set of futures that largely contribute to the anomalous deviation. In an alternative work, game theory was employed to offer a unified framework, namely SHAP [29], for interpreting predictions based on feature importance in supervised settings. Later, this technique was leveraged to provide additive explanation for anomalies detected by GRU-based autoencoder [15]. In the alternative approach, Wang et al. [46] used the reconstruction error's change ratio as an anomaly localization technique. The authors noticed that the complexity of the system requires a sounder technique for better attribution. Furthermore, Shalyga et al. [40] used the distance between the forecasted and the actual value of sensors' measurements to locate attacked tags at a certain point of time. The greatest error value in the prediction pointed out the attacked sensor.

Consideration 4: Given the ability of visual analytics to structure complex data, recognize patterns, and apprehend how individual elements are connected, we should plan the respective techniques to explain the incident and allow dynamic visual exploration.

Several advances have been made for the visualization of anomalies and multivariate data over time. Statistical diagrams, such as line charts and histograms, represent a widely used design that allows displaying anomalous tendencies in temporal data [23]. However, ICS consists of multiple assets; therefore, multiple lines in the same space reduce anomaly visibility. Thus, a glyph-based visual technique has gained more popularity due to its functional usage of screen space. It has been proven to be a practical technique to capture the behavior of individual users based on their communication activities over time [8]; it has been successfully used for computer network monitoring [22]. A spiral plot is another promising technique for monitoring ICS assets over time and letting visual analysis of the individual assets and their groups [27]. Finally, visual dashboards, similar to the one proposed in [5, 7], promote interactive investigation and provide diverse perspectives mainly centered around the system and its associated attack vector space.

Despite the advances above, several challenges pertain to the methods that rely exclusively on empirical data to support the detection of cyber threats.

Consideration 5: Spatial and temporal characteristics of data generated by ICS and its visibility present unique challenges that should be considered when planning data-driven attack detection methods.

The main motives for data secrecy refer to its operational sensitivity and the rarity of incident-related data. Indeed, providing open access to functional data enables the malicious actors to learn operational patterns that can be used for crafting highly stealthy attacks. In addition, the dependencies among measurements originated from spatial and temporal dimensions contradict the fundamental assumption of conventional data mining approaches that data instances are independent and identically distributed [4]. However, it is crucial to consider inherent dependencies among ICS assets to maintain adequate accuracy and attack localization level.

Furthermore, data heterogeneity both in space and in time is presented in various forms. Service distribution can follow a cyclical pattern in time; for instance, the amount of consumed electricity depends on the availability of natural light. Furthermore, ICS assets perform different functions: collect measurements or perform logical operations. In this context, empirical data can be presented as continuous or discrete variables.

Consideration 6: Given the high number of connected elements of ICS, it is critical to prioritize the examination of cyber misdemeanors by focusing on the attacked ICS assets first. Therefore, the next challenge herein is anomaly localization since mapping data anomalies to actual incidents for confirming cyber-attacks is nontrivial. Data patterns evolve at different levels due to the nonlinear and dynamic nature of ICS infrastructure.

In this context, data-driven methods, which learn the behavior of a single element of the system, explicitly determine the deviations for this particular asset; however, these methods fail to detect the coordinated attacks that affect the entire process. At the same time, the techniques that engage multivariate data portray a high level of false localizations. Therefore, the component of the situational awareness framework should strive for a balance between different perspectives to reduce false alarms and enhance operating efficiency.

Given the design considerations above, the cyber situational awareness framework for ICS should be able to perform the following actions:

- To evaluate the behavior of ICS assets without knowledge about its process model to address data availability challenges and model scalability (Design considerations 1, 2, and 5)
- To verify and demonstrate the status of ICS at different operational levels for the defined period to facilitate attack localization (Design considerations 3 and 6)
- To display warnings with all relevant details: incident overview and a detailed detection result (Design considerations 3 and 6)
- To monitor and provide visible alarm of cyber-attacks for critical ICS assets to support response prioritization (Design considerations 3 and 6)
- To assess the potential impact of a cyber incident to support an analytical interpretation (Design considerations 3, 4, and 6)
- To facilitate visual data comparison to support prompt decision-making and analytical interpretation (Design consideration 4)
- To support browsing of relevant raw data to provide a sufficient level of details if clarification of incident is required (Design considerations 3, 4, and 6)

4.2.2 Detailed Design

In a nutshell, the proposed cyber situational awareness framework consists of five modules, which incorporate machine learning methods, the theory of belief functions, and dynamic visualization. These components work together to detect and localize cyber incidents and evaluate their possible effect on the individual asset and ICS system.

Module 1 is designed to gather insights into ICS assets' behavioral patterns under attack-free operation. Module 2 takes the operational data as an input and estimates the irregularity score by comparing the incoming data series for each ICS asset with the expected system behavior that the model discovered in Module 1. A score that exceeds the predefined threshold indicates a cyber incident. Module 3 assesses the weight of each variable (ICS asset) in the irregularity score and pinpoints the exploited assets. Subsequently, Module 4 estimates the attack impact on ICS by employing algorithms rooted in resilience metrics. Finally, Module 5 maps analytical results to diverse appropriate visual techniques and interactions and generates a dynamic visual representation of cyber-attacks. This visual model supports evidence-based decisions. The role of a cyber analyst herein is to configure the system initially and conduct a meticulous analysis to determine the output validity and effectiveness of the integrated components. Figure 4.2 illustrates the framework pipeline.

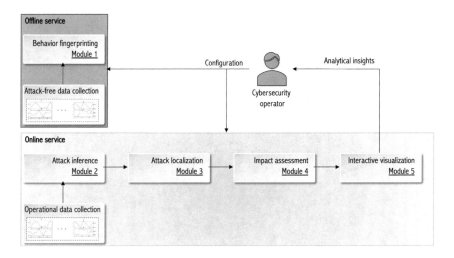

Fig. 4.2 The pipeline of the proposed cyber situational awareness framework for ICS

To achieve desired goals and address challenges, each module incorporates numerous techniques.

- Modules 1 and 2 employ a deep learning architecture that uses data that is automatically recorded by the ICS historian to learn and generalize operational patterns (Module 1) and detect deviations should ones occur (Module 2). Specifically, the approach leverages Generative Adversarial Networks (GANs), one of the machine learning algorithms widely used for anomaly detection across different domains such as healthcare, public safety, finance, and cybersecurity. The framework extends the application of GAN-based anomaly inference methods toward cybersecurity in critical infrastructure such as ICS deployed in smart cities.

- Module 3 localizes the incidents by employing three feature importance algorithms to derive the relative feature importance from the anomaly inference model. The latter is possible since the anomaly localization can be made with feature (ICS assets) selection algorithms [44]. The motivation behind converging diverse algorithms is that the independent results can be misinterpreted [44]. On the other hand, the combination presumably renders a better interpretation of the anomaly score. To this end, a fusion exploits a degree of a belief that the individual method correctly identifies an asset under attack.

- Module 4 exploits resilience metrics to calculate the impact of the cyber incident on the ICS operation. To ensure prompt estimation, the resilience metrics are calculated for the ICS assets that demonstrate abnormal behavior. It is essential to acknowledge that the effectiveness of the used metrics depends on attack intention; therefore, it is critical to have a substantial understanding of the

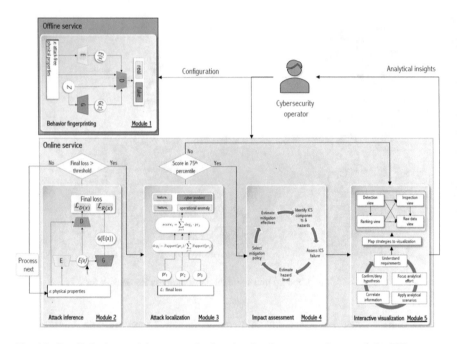

Fig. 4.3 Detailed scheme of the proposed cyber situational awareness framework for ICS

potential threats upfront implementation and take their evolution into account during continuous improvement.

- Module 5 applies various analytical strategies and maps visual techniques such as various charts (e.g., radar, bar, and line), color schemes, and diagrams to the anomaly detection and impacts estimation results to engage a cognitive apprehension of the ongoing incident. The module explores a system-theoretic approach to exercise the necessary extent for visual analysis to support the decision-making process with the entire system in mind.

Figure 4.3 illustrates the detailed architecture of the proposed cyber situational awareness framework for ICS deployed in smart cities.

4.2.2.1   Module 1: Behavior Fingerprinting

A plethora of machine learning techniques is suggested for effective pattern recognition and detection of rare instances in datasets. Being extremely data greedy, such algorithms require a large amount of data to train and test the model. Manipulating such big data, however, does not necessarily mean that the presence of unusual events will increase. The latter can reduce the effectiveness of the learner because it does not discriminate between the outliers and usual instances. The overlooked irregular events can have various impacts. The pointed challenges

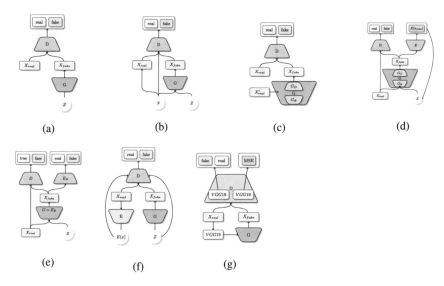

Fig. 4.4 Popular GAN architectures. (**a**) Original GAN. (**b**) CGAN. (**c**) pix2pix GAN. (**d**) GANomaly. (**e**) AAE. (**f**) BiGAN. (**g**) mGAN

motivate researchers to find techniques that can effectively learn patterns in data, distinguish abnormal instances, and address the irregularity of unusual events during the learning process. To address this challenge, the framework employs a Generative Adversarial Network (GAN) to fingerprint system behavior under regular operation.

Background: Generative Adversarial Networks for Anomaly Detection
When Goodfellow introduced Generative Adversarial Networks (GANs) [17], it had an instant and profound effect on the field. GANs consist of two competing neural network models, namely generator (G) and discriminator (D). The learning goal of a generator is to produce more realistic examples, while the discriminator aims at improving its ability to distinguish fake data from real. By leveraging a competition between two networks, which are trained simultaneously, the framework enables generation of instances that are almost indistinguishable from actual data. To unlock the potential of GANs and address their challenges, several extensions of the original framework have been designed and proposed in the literature. This section introduces these variants, starting from the initially proposed model.

The original GANs were proposed by Goodfellow [17]. In general, the GANs consist of two neural networks, namely a generator (G) and a discriminator (D). These networks compete for each other. The generator produces data instances, while the discriminator determines its authenticity. Figure 4.4a illustrates the architecture of the original version of GAN. As a first step, the generator receives noise z, to learn a distribution p_z. Based on the perceived distribution, the generator G produces data samples and passes them to the discriminator D. The discriminator then uses the Jensen–Shannon divergence to determine the distribution between real and fake data and back-propagate the probability of data authenticity to G. The generator subsequently adapts its parameters based on received gradient information and passes new samples to D. The learning goal of a generator is to produce more realistic examples, while the discriminator aims at improving its ability to distinguish fake data from real. These competing goals can be formalized as the following minimax game with value function V (G, D):

$$\min_{G} \max_{D} V(D, G) = \mathbb{E}_{x \sim p_{data}(x)}[\log(D(x))] + \mathbb{E}_{z \sim p_z(z)}[\log(1 - D(G(z)))]$$

(4.1)

where p_{data} is data distribution and p_z is the prior distribution of the generative network.

Challenges Although GANs demonstrated an ability to capture the modes of distribution, they face several challenges, such as (i) *training instability*, (ii) *mode collapse*, and (iii) *lack of practical measurements*. *Training instability* refers to the non-convergence of the model. Finding the equilibrium to the generator and discriminator game is the requirement of the GANs. In practice, many models cannot reach the equilibrium point. *Mode collapse* occurs when the generator learns to map several different noise input z values to the same output point [16]. It can happen because the maximin solution to the GAN game is different from the minimax solution (Eq. 4.2).

$$\min_{G} \max_{D} V(D, G) \neq \max_{D} \min_{G} V(D, G)$$

(4.2)

Given this problem, GANs are useful only for models that produce a small number of distinct instances [16]. The *lack of practical measurements* refers to the immaturity of stop indicators and evaluation criteria for effective comparison performance of various models [28].

Deep Convolutional GANs (DCGANs) A deep convolutional GAN (DCGAN) [35] trains a pair of deep convolutional generator and discriminator networks. A guideline for a stable DCGAN consists of a number of the specific attributes. For instance, a batch normalization layers are recommended for use in both networks to stabilize training in deeper models. Fully connected hidden layers are suggested for removal. Applying LeakyReLU activation function for all layers of the discriminator has been shown to improve the performance of the model. The stability of the DCGANs motivated researchers to widely employ this variant to their works. However, this architecture is still prone to mode collapse.

Wasserstein-GAN (WGAN) Wasserstein Distance, known as Earth Mover's distance, estimates the interval between two probability distributions. It provides a smooth representation of the distance even when two distributions are located in lower dimensional manifolds without overlaps. By leveraging this ability, Arjovsky et al. [3] proposed the Wasserstein-GAN (WGAN) architecture to stabilize GAN training and address mode collapse.

While the original model utilized the Jensen–Shannon divergence to determine the distribution between real and generated data, WGAN employs Wasserstein distance. Both generator and discriminator are presented as conventional DCGAN architecture. WGAN significantly advanced stability of GAN training, while it can lead to a slow optimization process.

Conditional GANs GANs are also extended to conditional GANs (CGANs) [31], which employ boundaries within which a generator can create the samples. In particular, the generator and the discriminator have specific conditions in the form of additional information y, which can be a class label. Presented as an additional vector, this information gets fed into both the discriminator and generator networks, and boosts the ability of GANs to generate instances with required attributes. The CGANs architecture can be visualized as a graph in Fig. 4.4b. The generator receives input noise z in combination with hidden representation y. In the discriminator, the input consists of x and y. In other words, $D(x, y)$ and $G(z, y)$ are conditioned to two variables, z or x and y. This model addresses both training stability and mode collapse.

Mathematically, the objective function of a two-player minimax game is

$$\min_G \max_D V(D, G) = \mathbb{E}_{x \sim p_{data}(x)}[\log(D(x|y))] + \mathbb{E}_{z \sim p_z(z)}[\log(1 - D(G(z|y)))]$$
(4.3)

CGANs were found to be able to provide better representations for multimodal data generation.

pix2pix Another inspiring model, named pix2pix [20], generalizes image-to-image translation tasks by employing CGANs. The conceptual design is illustrated in Fig. 4.4c. The input images condition the generator G, so that the generated samples follow the specific structure. Such a conditioning leads to a general improvement of the model. The generator uses an encoder–decoder with skip connections in the mirrored layers. The latter is known as U-Net [37]. To lower image blurring, $L1$ distance is used over $L2$ between generated samples. A convolutional PatchGAN [24] classifier, which only penalizes structure at the scale of image patches, was employed for the discriminator. An advantage of employing PathGAN is rooted in its ability to be applied to large images. The model demonstrated remarkable results in translating the black-and-white sketches to colored photos.

GANomaly Another GAN-based architecture used for anomaly detection was proposed by Akcay et al. [2]. The model, GANomaly, consists of three sub-networks. The first is generator G which leverages the autoencoder to learn and reconstruct the input data representation through the encoder and decoder, respectively. The encoder E is a convolutional network with batch-norm and a

LeakyRelu activation function, while a decoder consists of convolutional transpose layers, ReLU activation, and batch-norm. The second sub-network is an encoder that learns a representation of generated by G samples. The third network is the discriminator D with an architecture similar to a discriminator of DCGAN. The computational complexity of this model is significantly less than other GAN-based anomaly detection techniques.

Markovian GAN To increase time efficiency of generation of high-quality images, Li and Wand [24] proposed Markovian GAN, the conceptual model of which is illustrated in Fig. 4.4g. The key difference of the approach from original GANs is that it operates image patches rather than actual images. To this end, both generator and discriminator of this model are pre-trained VGG_19 networks [41]. In addition, a max-margin criteria (Hinge loss) replaces *sigmoid* function. Such the architecture is supposed to avoid mode collapse. The discriminator learns to distinguish actual feature patches from synthesized by the generator. Markovian GAN produces remarkable visual results.

Adversarial Autoencoders (AAEs) An autoencoder consists of two neural networks, an encoder E_E and a decoder E_D. It maps the input to latent space and remaps back to input data space. In the first step of adversarial autoencoder training, an encoder receives real data samples X_{real} as an input. E_E passes its output in the form of a latent code to a decoder for evaluation. The autoencoder is trained to reduce a reconstruction loss. The second step of adversarial autoencoder training aims to strengthen the discriminator. D takes as an input the output of E_E (which is the model generator G) and noise Z as input. The generator then adapts its parameters based on received gradient information and passes new samples to D. Training autoencoders with adversarial settings [30] improves reconstruction and increases control over latent vectors.

BiGAN Another extension of the original GAN model, named Bidirectional GAN (BiGAN) [11], is illustrated in Fig. 4.4f. In addition to the generator G, the architecture includes an encoder E which learns a feature space of underlying data $x = \{x_1, \ldots x_t\}$, where x_t denotes an m-dimensional vector $\{x_t^1, \ldots x_t^m\}$ representing sensor readings and actuator states at certain points of time. E maps x to latent variable space z. D discriminates data space x versus $G(z)$ and also $(x, E(x))$ versus $(G(z), z)$. In this architecture, an encoder E should learn to invert the generator G. The encoder cannot discover the output of the generator and vice versa. The simultaneous training of an encoder with generator and discriminator improves the robustness of the model. The optimization problem of this architecture is defined in Eq. 4.4.

$$\min_{G,E} \max_{D} V(D, E, G) = \mathbb{E}_{q(x)}[\log(D(x, E(x)))] + \mathbb{E}_{z \sim p(z)}[\log(1 - D(G(z), z))]$$

$$(4.4)$$

To train a strong discriminator, the architecture, namely *FakeGAN* [1], doubled the discriminator. To avoid model instability, D serves as a semi-supervised classifier. This model targets a text classification task. In particular, it was implemented to detect the deceptive web reviews. The first discriminator D aims to distinguish between truthful and misleading reviews, whereas the goal of the second discriminator D_1 is to generate fake samples by learning from the real false examples. During pre-training, Maximum Likelihood Estimation (MLE) is used to train G, which receives as an input the deceptive reviews. The generator G is defined as a stochastic policy model in reinforcement learning and is taught using Monte Carlo (MC) search. Furthermore, the generated instances along with real reviews are passed to the discriminator for classification. The model demonstrated its ability to address training instability and mode collapse.

Selected Model
The design components of the proposed behavioral fingerprinting (Fig. 4.5) are inspired by BiGAN [12].

This architecture was originally employed for anomaly detection in images. This work extends its application to data with temporal components and adjusts the underlying learning networks accordingly.

Fig. 4.5 Underlying deep learning architecture for behavior fingerprinting

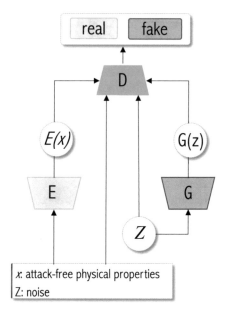

Input:
$x = \{x_1, \dots x_t\}$ - feature space (ICS asset measurements);
$x_t = \{x_t^1, \dots x_t^m\}$ - measurements at certain time;
for *number of training iterations* **do**

  for *k step* **do**

  $z_{fake} \leftarrow$ random samples
  $x_{fake} = G(z_{fake})$
  $z_{real} = E(x_{real})$
  Update $D([x_{fake}, z_{fake}])$ and $D([x_{real}, z_{real}])$ by maximizing (4.4)

  end

  $z_{fake} \leftarrow$ random samples
  $x_{fake} = G(z_{fake})$
  Update $G(z_{fake})$ and $E(x_{fake})$ by minimizing (4.4)

end

Algorithm 1: Training architecture for behavior fingerprinting

In addition to the generator G, the architecture includes an encoder E which learns a feature space of underlying data $x = \{x_1, \dots x_t\}$, where x_t denotes an m-dimensional vector $\{x_t^1, \dots x_t^m\}$ representing sensor readings and actuator states at certain points of time. E maps x to latent variable space z. D discriminates data space x versus $G(z)$ and also $(x, E(x))$ versus $(G(z), z)$. In this architecture, an encoder E should learn to invert the generator G. The encoder cannot discover the output of the generator and vice versa. The simultaneous training of an encoder with generator and discriminator improves the robustness of the model.

The training architecture for behavior fingerprinting is illustrated in Algorithm 1.

The building blocks of the learning components incorporate Recurrent Neural Network (RNN) and Convolution Neural Network (CNN). This combination leverages the ability of RNN to effectively grasp time series since it keeps track of previous data points and can perceive the long-term pattern. Besides, it exercises the power of CNN to learn features of time series and extract behavioral patterns.

4.2.2.2   Module 2: Attack Inference

Given the simultaneous training of D and G, it is advantageous to exploit both networks for attack detection, as suggested in [39]. Figure 4.6 illustrates the underlying architecture of inference model.

First, the approach utilizes the ability of trained D to distinguish the normal operational behavior of ICS. To this end, D determines the distribution between fingerprinted behavior and a latent representation of incoming data $E(x)$ and returns the abnormality score, namely the discriminator loss $\mathcal{L}_D(x)$ (Eq. 4.5).

$$\mathcal{L}_D(x) = cross\_entropy(D(x, E(x)), 1) \tag{4.5}$$

Fig. 4.6 Underlying deep learning architecture for anomaly inference

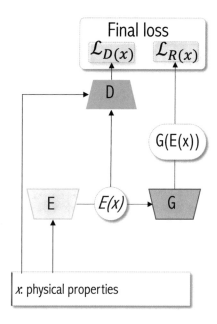

Furthermore, a network G is trained to capture the complexity of the data distribution and generate ICS assets' measurements and states at a certain point of time. Therefore, G can take a latent representation of incoming data obtained from the encoder and reconstruct the expected ICS behavior $(G(E(x)))$. The trained model then evaluates l_1-norm distance, namely residual loss, between actual (x) and expected $G(E(x))$ physical measurements for all ICS assets (Eq. 4.6).

$$\mathcal{L}_R(x) = \parallel x - G(E(x)) \parallel_1 \tag{4.6}$$

The model then obtains the irregularity score $\mathcal{L}_F(x)$ for each time point as a weighted sum of $\mathcal{L}_R(x)$ and $\mathcal{L}_D(x)$ (Eq. 4.7)

$$\mathcal{L}_F(x) = (1 - \alpha) * \mathcal{L}_R(x) + \alpha * \mathcal{L}_D(x) \tag{4.7}$$

where α is a weighting parameter controlling the impact of the loss on the anomaly score. A larger score $\mathcal{L}_F(x)$ denotes the time points representing physical properties of ICS that do not align with the fingerprinted behavior and, therefore, portrays an anomaly.

The process results in a vector representing variable-wise error and the irregularity score for incoming time points. This vector herein referred to as *anomaly score*. The latter manifests the presence of a potential cyber incident.

4.2.2.3   Module 3: Attack Localization

The underlying architecture of the framework is rooted in the method that solely relies on empirical data. From the data perspective, dataset features denote the ICS assets; therefore, the framework can use feature importance algorithms for anomaly localization [44]. Figure 4.7 illustrates the underlying architecture of anomaly localization module.

Feature importance refers to a range of techniques that rank the input variables of a prediction model, revealing the relative significance of each feature for prediction. Numerous algorithms exist in the literature and practice, for instance, decision trees, game-theoretical models, and statistical correlation. However, the estimates of these methods cannot be precise, implying that they can misrepresent the situation. In this context, the combination of such techniques may produce better anomaly localization and overcome the uncertainty of individual methods.

To this end, the framework first uses several feature importance techniques to estimate the relative significance of each ICS asset in demonstrated irregular behavior. The results of these methods are recorded as $pr = \{pr_1, ...pr_j\}$, where i is a number of selected techniques and pr_j denotes an m-dimensional vector $\{pr_j^1, ..., pr_j^m\}$ representing importance of a feature m for the anomaly. The method further uses a notion of degree of belief (deg_j) that the technique j accurately estimated the importance of the features. This degree is computed based on

Fig. 4.7 Underlying deep learning architecture for anomaly inference

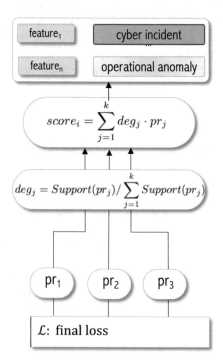

relative support [47] representing a distance between the estimations of participating methods.

$$deg_j = Support(pr_j) / \sum_{j=1}^{k} Support(pr_j) \qquad (4.8)$$

$$Support(pr_j) = \sum_{i=1, j \neq i}^{k} (1 - d(pr_i, pr_j)) \qquad (4.9)$$

Finally, for each variable m, the framework obtains the score representing a degree of contribution of the feature to the anomaly.

$$score_m = \sum_{j=1}^{k} deg_j \cdot pr_m \qquad (4.10)$$

As features represent ICS assets, an ICS asset is declared as an asset under attack if the $score_m$ of the respective variable is in the 75th percentile.

4.2.2.4 Module 4: Impact Assessment

The impact assessment of the cyber incident on ICS can be defined as five consequent actions [14]: (1) identify ICS assets and hazards, (2) assess ICS failure, (3) estimate hazard level, (4) select mitigation policy, and (5) estimate mitigation efficiency. Figure 4.8 illustrates the roadmap for assessing the impact of a cyber incident on the physical properties of the system.

Fig. 4.8 The roadmap for assessing the impact of a cyber incident on the system's physical properties

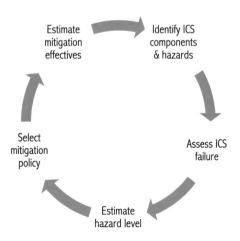

- **Step 1: Identify ICS assets and hazards.**
  This step aims to formally characterize the components and their dependencies to identify the hazards and control the adverse impact of the incident.
- **Step 2: Assess ICS failure.**
  The goal of the step is to assess the impact of identified hazards on the performance of the particular asset.
- **Step 3: Estimate hazard level.**
  The goal of this step is to enumerate the possible adverse scenarios and determine the potential severity of each. This step allows establishing the indicators that will be further compared against the situation during the incident to support effective resource allocation and selection of the appropriate response procedure.
- **Step 4: Select mitigation policy.**
  When the ICS asset demonstrates the possibility of failure due to a cyber incident, the next step is to identify potential mitigation measures and remove the ICS asset from the system or implement the procedures that make them recover faster.
- **Step 5: Estimate mitigation efficiency.**
  Once the mitigation options are defined, the next step is to evaluate whether they are efficient or not.

Following these steps, the framework first enumerates dependencies by employing the Pearson correlation coefficient ($corr_{xy}$) to the data collected by the ICS historian. This measurement, which formal definition is presented below, allows us to estimate and model how much the variables fluctuate together.

$$corr_{xy} = \frac{n \sum x_i y_i - \sum x_i \sum y_i}{\sqrt{n \sum x_i^2 - (\sum x_i)^2} \sqrt{n \sum y_i^2 - (\sum y_i)^2}} \qquad (4.11)$$

where x and y are two ICS assets, n is the number of observations, and i is ith observation.

The intentional (or result of unintentional) cyber incidents can vary from water tank underflow/overflow to system malfunctioning and degradation of water quality (e.g., chemical or biological.)

To identify the asset failure, the framework quantifies the physical response of the system by evaluating the loss of performance of each element. A framework employs various resilience metrics depending on the ICS functions formalized in step 1. In the presented case, the framework employed several metrics related to water treatment plant. The following indices, which are suggested in [43], estimate tank overflow/underflow status and effect.

The first index, $T_{underflow}$, evaluates the amount of time during which the water tank received a water volume that is below minimal:

$$T_{underflow} = \sum_{t=1}^{T} l_t \Delta t \qquad (4.12)$$

Herein, l_t is defined as

$$l_t = \begin{cases} 1, & h_t < l, \\ 0 & otherwise \end{cases} \quad (4.13)$$

where h_t is a water level of the tank under investigation and l is lower acceptable water level. This cyber incident can be evident in the physical damage to the system.

Similarly, $T_{overflow}$ is employed to evaluate the amount of time during which the water tank received a water volume that exceeds the maximum:

$$T_{overflow} = \sum_{t=1}^{T} l_t \Delta t \quad (4.14)$$

where

$$l_t = \begin{cases} 1, & h_t > u, \\ 0 & otherwise \end{cases} \quad (4.15)$$

and u is upper acceptable water level. This cyber incident can affect the equipment's physical status and result in the waste of water resources: spilled water will never be distributed to the residents.

Furthermore, $T_{undeflow}$ and $T_{overflow}$ are compared with predefined threshold θ_u and θ_o respectfully, to assign a corresponding level of incident severity.

$$level_{underflow} = \begin{cases} 1, & T_{underflow} < \theta_u, \\ 0 & otherwise \end{cases} \quad (4.16)$$

$$level_{overflow} = \begin{cases} 1, & T_{overflow} > \theta_o, \\ 0 & otherwise \end{cases} \quad (4.17)$$

The respective mitigation procedure should be employed for the cases with severity level 1. Furthermore, during the forensic investigation of the event, the mitigation strategy is evaluated based on recovery time from the incident, and the appropriate decision regarding its efficiency is made.

4.2.2.5 Module 5: Interactive Visualization

The results from the inference and impact quantification modules are passed to the interactive visualization module, where the domain expert can then analyze the suspected anomaly, decide whether a detected anomaly is a false alarm, or look for more information if it is impossible to reach a confident conclusion. To

Fig. 4.9 The components of
visual analytics

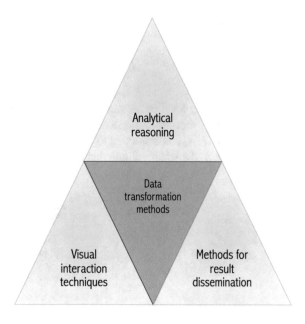

achieve this, the framework uses visual analytics (VA) that promotes the analytical reasoning process by maximizing the human capacity to perceive, interpret, and reason complex data and events. VA is a transdisciplinary field that involves several components, such as analytical reasoning, visual interaction techniques, data transformation methods, and various methods for result dissemination [45] (Fig. 4.9).

Analytical reasoning techniques allow obtaining the insights that directly support evaluation and decision-making. Visual interaction techniques leverage human cognition to recognize, explore, and interpret large amounts of information. Data transformation methods recast conflicting and dynamic data to a form that supports analysis. The methods for generating, presenting, and disseminating analytical results allow communication with an audience with diverse backgrounds. The framework first models domain-aware analytical reasoning and then maps it to the visual techniques, views, and appropriate interaction. Figure 4.10 illustrates the steps of analytical reasoning considered in this work.

Some unique aspects of analysis in this area include (i) inherited dependencies among subsystems and individual assets of ICS, and it signifies that the monitoring of individual ICS assets is insufficient, (ii) the need to separate actual facts from false alarms, and (iii) insights into how the physical environment can be affected. The module then maps the analytical strategies to visualization techniques. It explores a system-theoretic approach to exercise the necessary extent for visual analysis to support the decision-making process with the entire system in mind. The multidimensional representation allows prompt recognition of the anomalies in the system and gradually narrows the investigation.

Fig. 4.10 The roadmap for employing analytical reasoning

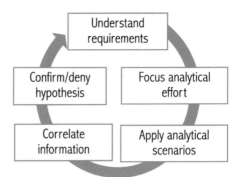

Specifically, the visual components consist of four interactive coordinated views:

- *Detection*. This view highlights the detected anomalies at the entire system during a selected time period (24 h). In the context of process levels, for each hour, a designed visual representation presents anomaly ranking and attacked/affected ICS assets with the confidence level that the ICS asset is affected.
- *Inspection*. This view highlights the inferred analytics details at various levels according to the developed analytical strategies.
- *Ranking*. This view provides rank of the selected anomalies. The rank includes an anomaly score and also the confidence level of the attribution of the attack to a specific process level and respective ICS asset.
- *Raw data*. This view illustrates raw data for the selected time and ICS asset.

All these views consist of various sub-views to cover analytical strategies. Rich interaction promotes data exploration and hypothesis testing.

Detection view (Fig. 4.11) aims to report the status across the ICS assets and to support the initial triage of the detected cyber incidents. Simultaneous monitoring of all ICS assets is vital for the systems with intrinsic dependencies.

The view has a circular structure with multiple levels that symbolize the process group. The circle is divided into areas depicting 15 min intervals that are also grouped into 1-h periods. The view reports the anomaly score as a bar diagram in the internal circle. The shaded circle denotes the predefined threshold for an anomaly; therefore, the analyst should investigate the reason if the bar hits a shady zone. The pulsation technique and color capture the analyst's attention to the critical assets.

Inspection view (Fig. 4.12) offers the details for the selected anomaly score.

The view has a network graph with the nodes symbolizing ICS assets grouped on the process level. ICS assets affected by the incidents are highlighted with a dark color, while the pulsation technique and brighter color pinpoint the critical asset to focus the investigation.

The edges of the graph depict the correlation between individual sensors and actuators. The strong correlation between ICS assets is represented using the weight

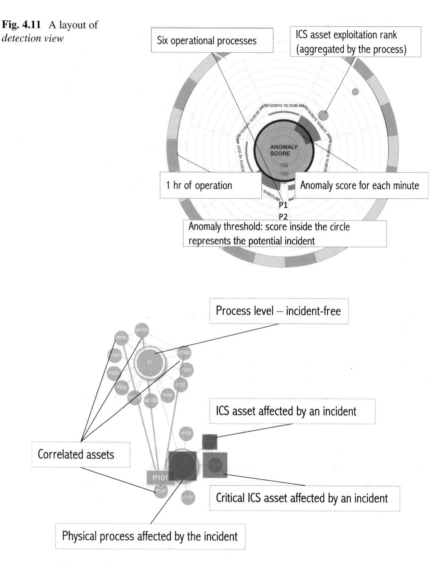

Fig. 4.11 A layout of *detection view*

Fig. 4.12 A layout of *detection view*

of the edges to provide more insights into the potential and actual impact of the ongoing incident.

Ranking view (Fig. 4.13) guides the investigation through several ranks that support evident-based prioritization.

The following measures are incorporated into the dashboard:

- ICS asset contribution to the anomaly given the relationship between system components (estimated as $score_m$ by the attribution algorithms)
- A physical system response on the incident

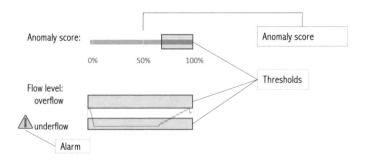

Fig. 4.13 A layout of *ranking view*

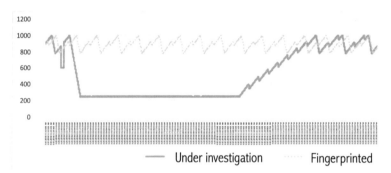

Fig. 4.14 A layout of *raw data view*

Predefined thresholds (shady areas) permit the focus solely on significant issues; if not significant, the value of the rank will not hit the shady area.

Raw data view (Fig. 4.14) displays the raw data collected by the individual asset and visually compares it with the fingerprinted system behavior.

The dynamic nature of the dashboard allows for filtering data and exploring data from general to specific characteristics. An analyst can use each view individually to test the hypothesis and identify false negatives.

4.3 Continuous Improvement: Evaluation Strategy

The following metrics are regularly evaluated to support the sustainability of the framework:

- Capability to fingerprint system behavior
- Ability to infer anomaly
- Capability to perform anomaly localization

The introduced framework heavily relies on the network's capability to capture the complexity of the data distribution. The ultimate usage of the generated sequences is to train a model to detect anomalies in the physical measurements of a water treatment plant. To evaluate how firmly the model does so, a discrepancy measure, known as Energy Distance (ED) [42], a statistic that is based on the idea that observations should have zero potential energy only if they originate from the same underlying distribution is employed. Mathematically,

$$ED(x, z)^2 = (2\mathbb{E}|X - Z| - \mathbb{E}|X - X'| - \mathbb{E}|Z - Z'|) \tag{4.18}$$

where X, X' and Z, Z' are independent random variables of original and forecasted physical properties, and x and z are their respective distribution. In addition, the framework uses the Maximum Mean Discrepancy (MMD), which has proven to be well suited to evaluate the quality of generated GAN samples in multivariate data [18]. Formally, MMD is defined as follows:

$$\widehat{MMD^2} = \frac{1}{n(n-1)} \sum_{j \neq j} k(x_i, x_j) + \frac{1}{n(n-1)} \sum_{j \neq j} k(z_i, z_j) - \frac{2}{n^2} \sum_{j,j} k(x_i, z_z) \tag{4.19}$$

A lower ED and MMD measures indicate the lower discrepancy between two probabilities and suggest, after stabilization, the high quality of behavioral fingerprinting.

The anomaly inference function performance is determined by testing its ability to detect the incident (with acceptable false alarms). To this end, it first measures the sensitivity (or recall), which is the proportion of the correctly inferred attack points to the total number of cases when the ICS is under attack. It is formally defined as $tp / (tp + fn)$. Hereafter, tp and tn stand for the number of true positives and true negatives, respectively; fp and fn denote the number of false positives and negatives. The framework further evaluates the precision, which measures the proportion of correctly identified attack of all the points that are classified as positive; it is formally defined as $tp / (tp + fp)$.

To evaluate the ability of the inference function to avoid false alarms, the framework estimates the specificity, which is the proportion of the correctly recognized non-attack points to all cases when the ICS is operating under a regular/normal operation cycle. Mathematically, it equates to $tn / (tn + fp)$. To test the accuracy of the model, it employs the typical F-measure, which represents the harmonic mean of the sensitivity and precision, and takes into account both false positive and false negative rates.

To assess the capability to perform anomaly localization, the method compares qualitative results with ground truth annotations from the attack log (in the empirical dataset). In addition, it compares precision, recall, and F-measure metrics obtained using the proposed approach and those that have been reported in the literature.

4.4 Summary

Despite the increasing number of malicious incidents, the main challenge of applying data analytics approaches related to the limited collection of previously inferred malicious events remains unsolved. Therefore, a situational awareness pipeline for ICS assets should generalize the underlying system and support inference of a wide range of cyber incidents without previous knowledge of the latter and provide accurate incident localization to effectively allocate response resources. Although numerous sound developments are presented in the literature, they rarely offer the essential strategy to localize the incident and quantify the impact. The latter, however, is a critical function toward proper mitigation and forensics prioritization as well as for the transition of situational awareness methods to operation.

To this end, this chapter offers a framework that integrates machine learning, the theory of belief functions, and dynamic visualization to coordinate the inference, localization and visual exploration of cyber incidents. The approach broads the analytical perspective and provides desired granularity and the interpretation of attack impact.

The framework is designed to work with multivariate data to exploit the inherent dependencies between ICS assets, leading to better anomaly inference. Furthermore, the underlying deep learning architecture learns system behavior and does not require previous knowledge about its process model. Besides, it can be trained using only attack-free instances; therefore, it manifests as a promising application in cybersecurity of ICS, where attack-related data is rarely available. Finally, it identifies the ICS assets that suffer from a cyber incident to focus resources and mitigation strategies. Moreover, the framework uniquely extends the application of the degree of belief functions to address uncertainties in anomaly localization.

Through the dynamic visualization, the presented framework shows the behavior and state of ICS at both local (individual assets) and global (all assets simultaneously) levels and effectively utilizes a screen space. It also promotes investigation of the implications of a cyber incident. A combination of the suggested analytical strategies and their respective dynamic visualization provides evidence of such effect and the basis for decision-making. The framework is designed to work with multivariate data to exploit the inherent dependencies between ICS assets, leading to better anomaly inference. Furthermore, the underlying deep learning architecture learns system behavior and does not require previous knowledge about its process model. Besides, it can be trained using only attack-free instances; therefore, it manifests as a promising application in cybersecurity of ICS, where attack-related data is rarely available. Finally, it identifies the ICS assets that suffer from a cyber incident to focus resources and mitigation strategies. Moreover, the framework uniquely extends the application of the degree of belief functions to address uncertainties in anomaly localization.

References

1. Hojjat Aghakhani, Aravind Machiry, Shirin Nilizadeh, Christopher Kruegel, and Giovanni Vigna. Detecting Deceptive Reviews using Generative Adversarial Networks. *arXiv preprint arXiv:1805.10364*, 2018.
2. Samet Akcay, Amir Atapour-Abarghouei, and Toby P Breckon. GANomaly: Semi-Supervised Anomaly Detection via Adversarial Training. *arXiv preprint arXiv:1805.06725*, 2018.
3. Martin Arjovsky, Soumith Chintala, and Léon Bottou. Wasserstein GAN. *arXiv preprint arXiv:1701.07875*, 2017.
4. Gowtham Atluri, Anuj Karpatne, and Vipin Kumar. Spatio-temporal data mining: A survey of problems and methods. *ACM Computing Surveys (CSUR)*, 51(4):1–41, 2018.
5. Georgios Bakirtzis, Brandon J Simon, Cody H Fleming, and Carl R Elks. Looking for a black cat in a dark room: Security visualization for cyber-physical system design and analysis. In *2018 IEEE Symposium on Visualization for Cyber Security (VizSec)*, pages 1–8. IEEE, 2018.
6. Elias Bou-Harb, Walter Lucia, Nicola Forti, Sean Weerakkody, Nasir Ghani, and Bruno Sinopoli. Cyber meets control: A novel federated approach for resilient cps leveraging real cyber threat intelligence. *IEEE Communications Magazine*, 55(5):198–204, 2017. Publisher: IEEE.
7. Elias Bou-Harb and Nataliia Neshenko. *Cyber Threat Intelligence for the Internet of Things*. Springer, 2020.
8. Nan Cao, Conglei Shi, Sabrina Lin, Jie Lu, Yu-Ru Lin, and Ching-Yung Lin. TargetVue: Visual analysis of anomalous user behaviors in online communication systems. *IEEE transactions on visualization and computer graphics*, 22(1):280–289, 2015.
9. Rohan Chabukswar, Yilin Mo, and Bruno Sinopoli. Detecting integrity attacks on SCADA systems. *IFAC Proceedings Volumes*, 44(1):11239–11244, 2011. Publisher: Elsevier.
10. CISA. CRR supplemental resource guide, volume 10: Situational awareness - CISA.
11. Jeff Donahue, Philipp Krähenbühl, and Trevor Darrell. Adversarial feature learning. *arXiv preprint arXiv:1605.09782*, 2016.
12. Jeff Donahue, Philipp Krähenbühl, and Trevor Darrell. Adversarial feature learning. *arXiv preprint arXiv:1605.09782*, 2016.
13. M. Elnour, N. Meskin, K. Khan, and R. Jain. A Dual-Isolation-Forests-Based Attack Detection Framework for Industrial Control Systems. *IEEE Access*, 8:36639–36651, 2020.
14. EPA. Creating resilient water utilities (CRWU).
15. Ioana Giurgiu and Anika Schumann. Additive Explanations for Anomalies Detected from Multivariate Temporal Data. In *Proceedings of the 28th ACM International Conference on Information and Knowledge Management*, pages 2245–2248, 2019.
16. Ian Goodfellow. NIPS 2016 Tutorial: Generative Adversarial Networks. *arXiv preprint arXiv:1701.00160*, 2016.
17. Ian Goodfellow, Jean Pouget-Abadie, Mehdi Mirza, Bing Xu, David Warde-Farley, Sherjil Ozair, Aaron Courville, and Yoshua Bengio. Generative Adversarial Nets. In *Advances in neural information processing systems*, pages 2672–2680, 2014.
18. Arthur Gretton, Karsten Borgwardt, Malte Rasch, Bernhard Schölkopf, and Alex J Smola. A kernel method for the two-sample-problem. In *Advances in neural information processing systems*, pages 513–520, 2007.
19. Jun Inoue, Yoriyuki Yamagata, Yuqi Chen, Christopher M Poskitt, and Jun Sun. Anomaly detection for a water treatment system using unsupervised machine learning. In *2017 IEEE international conference on data mining workshops (ICDMW)*, pages 1058–1065. IEEE, 2017.
20. Phillip Isola, Jun-Yan Zhu, Tinghui Zhou, and Alexei A Efros. Image-to-Image Translation with Conditional Adversarial Networks. *arXiv preprint*, 2017.
21. R. Khanna and H. Liu. Control theoretic approach to intrusion detection using a distributed hidden Markov model. *IEEE Wireless Communications*, 15(4):24–33, 2008.

22. Igor V Kotenko, Maxim Kolomeets, Andrey Chechulin, and Yannick Chevalier. A visual analytics approach for the cyber forensics based on different views of the network traffic. *J. Wirel. Mob. Networks Ubiquitous Comput. Dependable Appl.*, 9(2):57–73, 2018.

23. Pavel Laskov, Konrad Rieck, Christin Schäfer, and Klaus-Robert Müller. Visualization of anomaly detection using prediction sensitivity. *Sicherheit 2005, Sicherheit–Schutz und Zuverlässigkeit*, 2005.

24. Chuan Li and Michael Wand. Precomputed Real-Time Texture Synthesis with Markovian Generative Adversarial Networks. In *European Conference on Computer Vision*, pages 702–716. Springer, 2016.

25. Dan Li, Dacheng Chen, Baihong Jin, Lei Shi, Jonathan Goh, and See-Kiong Ng. MAD-GAN: Multivariate anomaly detection for time series data with generative adversarial networks. In *International Conference on Artificial Neural Networks*, pages 703–716. Springer, 2019.

26. Qin Lin, Sridha Adepu, Sicco Verwer, and Aditya Mathur. TABOR: A graphical model-based approach for anomaly detection in industrial control systems. In *Proceedings of the 2018 on Asia Conference on Computer and Communications Security*, pages 525–536, 2018.

27. Anna-Pia Lohfink, Simon D Duque Anton, Hans Dieter Schotten, Heike Leitte, and Christoph Garth. Security in process: visually supported triage analysis in industrial process data. *IEEE transactions on visualization and computer graphics*, 26(4):1638–1649, 2020.

28. Mario Lucic, Karol Kurach, Marcin Michalski, Sylvain Gelly, and Olivier Bousquet. Are GANs created equal? a large-scale study. In *Advances in neural information processing systems*, pages 697–706, 2018.

29. Scott M Lundberg and Su-In Lee. A unified approach to interpreting model predictions. In *Advances in neural information processing systems*, pages 4765–4774, 2017.

30. Alireza Makhzani, Jonathon Shlens, Navdeep Jaitly, Ian Goodfellow, and Brendan Frey. Adversarial autoencoders. *arXiv preprint arXiv:1511.05644*, 2015.

31. Mehdi Mirza and Simon Osindero. Conditional generative adversarial nets. *arXiv preprint arXiv:1411.1784*, 2014.

32. Y. Mo, S. Weerakkody, and B. Sinopoli. Physical Authentication of Control Systems: Designing Watermarked Control Inputs to Detect Counterfeit Sensor Outputs. *IEEE Control Systems Magazine*, 35(1):93–109, 2015.

33. Nataliia Neshenko, Christelle Nader, Elias Bou-Harb, and Borko Furht. A survey of methods supporting cyber situational awareness in the context of smart cities. *Journal of Big Data*, 7(1):1–41, 2020. Publisher: SpringerOpen.

34. Fabio Pasqualetti, Florian Dörfler, and Francesco Bullo. Attack detection and identification in cyber-physical systems. *IEEE transactions on automatic control*, 58(11):2715–2729, 2013. Publisher: IEEE.

35. Alec Radford, Luke Metz, and Soumith Chintala. Unsupervised representation learning with deep convolutional generative adversarial networks. *arXiv preprint arXiv:1511.06434*, 2015.

36. Marco Tulio Ribeiro, Sameer Singh, and Carlos Guestrin. " Why should I trust you?" Explaining the predictions of any classifier. In *Proceedings of the 22nd ACM SIGKDD international conference on knowledge discovery and data mining*, pages 1135–1144, 2016.

37. Olaf Ronneberger, Philipp Fischer, and Thomas Brox. U-Net: Convolutional Networks for Biomedical Image Segmentation. In *International Conference on Medical image computing and computer-assisted intervention*, pages 234–241. Springer, 2015.

38. Eduardo Salas, Carolyn Prince, David P Baker, and Lisa Shrestha. Situation awareness in team performance: Implications for measurement and training. *Human factors*, 37(1):123–136, 1995.

39. Thomas Schlegl, Philipp Seeböck, Sebastian M Waldstein, Ursula Schmidt-Erfurth, and Georg Langs. Unsupervised Anomaly Detection with Generative Adversarial Networks to Guide Marker Discovery. In *International Conference on Information Processing in Medical Imaging*, pages 146–157. Springer, 2017.

40. Dmitry Shalyga, Pavel Filonov, and Andrey Lavrentyev. Anomaly detection for water treatment system based on neural network with automatic architecture optimization. *arXiv preprint arXiv:1807.07282*, 2018.

41. Karen Simonyan and Andrew Zisserman. Very Deep Convolutional Networks for Large-Scale Image Recognition. *arXiv preprint arXiv:1409.1556*, 2014.
42. Gábor J Székely and Maria L Rizzo. Energy statistics: A class of statistics based on distances. *Journal of statistical planning and inference*, 143(8):1249–1272, 2013. Publisher: Elsevier.
43. Riccardo Taormina, Stefano Galelli, Nils Ole Tippenhauer, Elad Salomons, and Avi Ostfeld. Characterizing cyber-physical attacks on water distribution systems. *Journal of Water Resources Planning and Management*, 143(5):04017009, 2017.
44. Riccardo Taormina, Stefano Galelli, Nils Ole Tippenhauer, Elad Salomons, Avi Ostfeld, Demetrios G Eliades, Mohsen Aghashahi, Raanju Sundararajan, Mohsen Pourahmadi, M Katherine Banks, and others. Battle of the attack detection algorithms: Disclosing cyber attacks on water distribution networks. *Journal of Water Resources Planning and Management*, 144(8):04018048, 2018. Publisher: American Society of Civil Engineers.
45. James J Thomas and Kristin A Cook. A visual analytics agenda. *IEEE computer graphics and applications*, 26(1):10–13, 2006.
46. Chao Wang, Bailing Wang, Hongri Liu, and Haikuo Qu. Anomaly Detection for Industrial Control System Based on Autoencoder Neural Network. *Wireless Communications and Mobile Computing*, 2020, 2020. Publisher: Hindawi.
47. Deng Yong, Shi Wenkang, Zhu Zhenfu, and Liu Qi. Combining belief functions based on distance of evidence. *Decision support systems*, 38(3):489–493, 2004. Publisher: Elsevier.

Chapter 5
Case Study: Situational Awareness for Water Treatment Systems

Cyber-attacks on water facilities, including water treatment plants, water distribution systems, or wastewater utility companies, can cause significant damage and endanger the well-being of citizens. The attacks against water systems have several dimensions, such as physical damage and chemical or biological hazards, which can have social and financial implications. A particular case of cyber-attacks that manipulate sensor data without violation of the control flow integrity of ICS represents the new frontier of cyber threat. Given that many control decisions depend on specific measurements of ICS assets, this type of cyber event can cause severe harm to mechanical systems. Plant operators must understand the response of ICS to a variety of targeted attacks for a prompt and proper response and further system adaptation to protect it from such types of attacks.

This chapter recaps the history of cyber incidents against water systems in Sect. 5.1 and conveys the significance of cyber situational awareness in this environment. To this end, this chapter offers a business case of application (Sect. 5.2) of the framework introduced in Chap. 4 to the small-scale water treatment plant [3], similar to those found in small cities.

5.1   History of Attacks Against Water Infrastructure

5.1.1   Israel's Water System Attack

Incident   In 2020, an attacker terrorized Israel's water system by conducting two cyber-attacks. One of the attacks targeted agricultural water pumps in the upper Galilee. Another one hit infrastructure in the center of the country and aimed at increasing chlorine levels in water flowing to residential areas. The water authority confirmed the incidents, assuring that no damage was done to Israel's water system [14].

© The Author(s), under exclusive license to Springer Nature Switzerland AG 2022
N. Neshenko et al., *Smart Cities: Cyber Situational Awareness to Support Decision Making*, https://doi.org/10.1007/978-3-031-18464-2_5

Lessons Learned The incident confirmed one more time that the landscape of the targets of cyber-attacks in water systems is wide and may include water treatment and irrigation systems.

5.1.2 Onslow Water and Sewer Company Hack

Background Onslow Water and Sewer Authority, a water utility company in Jacksonville (North Carolina) [19] that serves about 54,744 water and 7221 sewer accounts.

Incident In October 2018, Onslow Water and Sewer Company fell victim to a ransomware attack [13]. The attack began by spreading a virus known as EMOTET; the virus was detected by the company team and passed for investigation by security experts outside the company. However, an attacker did not lose valuable time and launched a more sophisticated virus known as RYUK. Although the response team immediately disconnected the facility from the Internet, the virus reached its goal and encrypted data. Following encryption, the authorities received an email demanding payment to unlock data. Criminals did not receive payment since the company refused to negotiate.

Lessons Learned Ransomware is a fast-growing threat, targeting users of all types, and smart cities are not excluded. A proper mechanism should be introduced to protect critical infrastructure from this threat.

5.1.3 Kemuri Water Company

Background An undisclosed water utility in the USA, shown under the pseudonym of Kemuri Water Company.

Incident In 2016, an attacker gained access to a control application responsible for manipulating hundreds of PLCs of the undisclosed water treatment plant [17]. Furthermore, an attacker altered the number of induced chemicals and affected water treatment and production capabilities. According to Verizon, a Syria hacktivist group was behind the attack. The Kemuri attack can have a catastrophic effect on the community. Subsequently, a comprehensive assessment was conducted on both operational technologies and information systems. It revealed numerous vulnerabilities with a high-risk level, including one that is related to the reliance on outdated computers and operating systems.

Lessons Learned The incident pinpointed the necessity of several strategies that can protect ICS deployed in critical infrastructure from cyber-attacks. Among others, having Internet-facing ICSs is a flawed practice for critical infrastructure due to the consequences on society.

5.1.4   The Maroochy Water Services Attack

Background   Maroochy Shire is a small town in Queensland, Australia, with about 130,000 residents. The Maroochy Shire Council runs the Sewage Treatment Plant that daily treats 10 million gallons of sewage. The plant operates Supervisory Control and Data Acquisition (SCADA) system to control about 142 sewage pumping stations deployed around the town.

Incident   Between 9 February 2000 and 23 April 2000, the SCADA experienced faults, ranging from communication and pump control capabilities loss to false alarms and altered configuration of the pumping stations. An adversary gained remote access to the computers controlling the Maroochy Shire Council's sewerage system and altered data sensed by particular sewerage pumping stations, resulting in the malfunction of their operations. Over this period, an attacker released about 1 million liters of untreated sewage into a stormwater drain from where it flowed to local parks, rivers, and residential grounds. The motivation behind the attack was revenge on a former employee after he failed to secure his job with Maroochy Shire Council.

Lessons Learned   The skilled attacker with insider knowledge used his access credentials after being fired. This incident stresses the need for sound access management procedures that include the rigid process of access revoking.

5.2   Cyber Situation Awareness for Water Treatment Plant

A water treatment testbed (Fig. 5.1), known as Secure Water Treatment (SWaT), was launched on 18 Mar 2015 by Chief Defence Scientist Prof. Quek Tong Boon to support research in the area of cyber security [3]. Since then, it has served as a fundamental asset for researchers in Singapore and worldwide, seeking to design secure CPS.

5.2.1   Cyber-Physical Process Overview

Figure 5.2 formally introduces six stages of the treatment process of the SWaT testbed.

Fig. 5.1 SWaT: Secure Water Treatment Testbed [9]

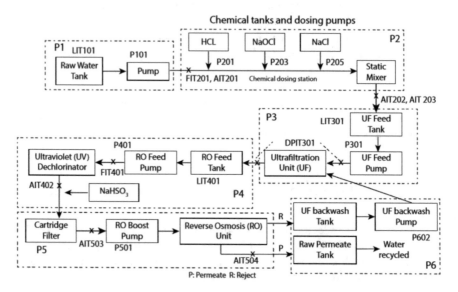

Fig. 5.2 SWaT testbed process overview. Process 1 though Process 6 pinpoint the six stages of the treatment process [3]

In particular, the physical treatment process begins by taking in raw water, following by adding required chemicals to it and then filtering it via an Ultrafiltration (UF) system. Furthermore, UV lamps de-chlorinate water and pass it to a Reverse Osmosis (RO) system. A backwash process cleans the membranes in UF using the water produced by RO. Figure 5.3 summarizes the details of the processes.

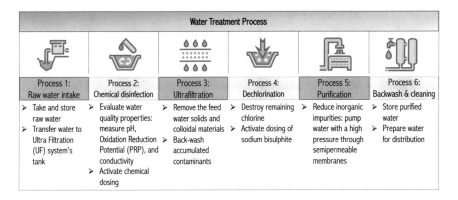

Fig. 5.3 SWaT: Physical process overview

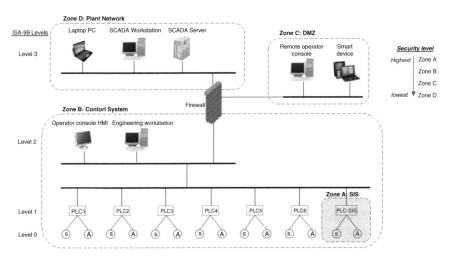

Fig. 5.4 SWaT: Network architecture [3]

A layered communication network along with Programmable Logic Controllers (PLCs), Supervisory Control and Data Acquisition (SCADA) workstation, a Historian, and Human Machine Interfaces (HMIs) forms a cyber portion of SWaT. The overall network architecture of SWaT is illustrated in Fig. 5.4. The testbed consists of two different communication channels: wired (IEEE 802.3 Ethernet) and wireless (IEEE 802.11). Each stage of water process treatment is controlled by PLC, which is connected to SCADA and to sensors and actuators. The latter is connected through individual Fieldbus rings.

The role of PLC is to receive the information from the corresponding sensors and compute the control actions to the actuators. In addition, data from sensors is available to the SCADA system and recorded by the historian to support subsequent analysis.

5.2.2 Dataset Overview

The SWaT dataset consists of collected physical properties that include sensor measurements (25 continuous variables) and actuators' states (26 discrete variables). A vital feature of the dataset collected with an operating horizon of eleven days is the absence of cyber-attacks during the first seven days. This quality makes it suitable for examining data patterns generated by the ICS assets under normal operating conditions.

In addition, the dataset consists of four working days under different cyber-attacks that targeted one or multiple ICS assets in various process stages and were carefully labeled.

The primary data characteristics of the dataset generated by SWaT testbed are summarized in Table 5.1.

5.2.2.1 Attack Scenarios

The following classes of the attacks are carefully labeled in dataset.

- Single-Stage Single-Point (SSSP) attack targets exactly one ICS asset.
- Single-Stage Multi-Point (SSMP) attack aims at several ICS assets deployed on one process level.
- Multi-Stage Single-Point (MSSP) attack is performed on multiple stages and targets exactly one asset at each process level.
- Multi-Stage Multi-Point (MSMP) attack is performed on two or more ICS process levels and targets multiple assets at each of them.

The attack intentions vary from tank overflow/underflow, reduced water quality, and system malfunctioning. Figure 5.5 shows the distribution of the attack purpose across their classes.

The duration of these attacks varies from 100 s to 10 h. While system requires time for recover after an attack, the exact time is not provided in the dataset description.

From the analysis of the cyber incidents in the water sector [4], the following intention of the attacker can be distinguished: cause overflow and underflow in the

Table 5.1 The characteristics of SWaT dataset

Characteristics	Value
Variables	51
Instances in dataset	
Attack-free operation	496,800
Data with attacks	449,919
Number of attacks	36
Attack duration	100 s–10 h

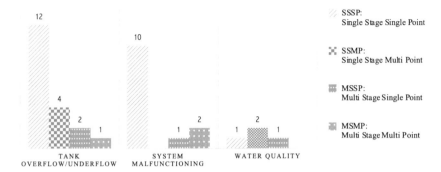

Fig. 5.5 Distribution of the attack intention across the attack classes

tanks, reduce the quality of the water, damage the critical components of ICS, shut down the plant, or reduce the distribution level of purified water.

Furthermore, depending on the attacker's knowledge of the specification of each sensor and actuator, the complexity of the attack can also vary. For instance, without prior knowledge of the system dynamic, the adversary can send a direct command to the actuator to manipulate the system's current state. A more complex attack can include the injection of false measurements, which are dynamically calculated by ICS, to trigger an incorrect response of the PLC and lead undesired system state.

The following data preprocessing procedure is conducted. First, the initial 6 h from the training (attack-free) dataset, representing system stabilization which can affect the behavioral fingerprinting task, are trimmed. Then the original dataset is scaled to optimize computation so that every attribute had a mean value of 0 and a standard deviation of 1.

5.2.3   Operational Patterns Examination

As a provision for anomaly detection, the machine learning technique should precisely recognize operational behavioral patterns of the system under attack-free operation [10]. Therefore, the two following prerequisites should be satisfied to guarantee a sufficient performance.

- The training process of deep learning architecture should continue until the model demonstrates high performance in learning.
- The deep learning architecture should precisely perceive sensor readings' distribution.

Following the framework introduced in Chap. 4, discrepancy measures, known as Energy Distance (ED) [15] and Maximum Mean Discrepancy (MMD), are employed to ensure that the learning process of deployed architecture continues until the model demonstrates high performance in learning. Both ED and MMD

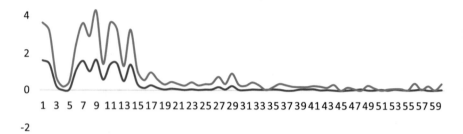

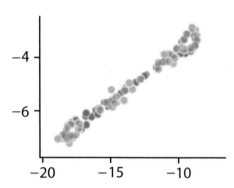

Fig. 5.6 Maximum mean discrepancy (MMD) and energy distance (ED) as a function of learning epoch [10]

Fig. 5.7 t-SNE visualization: original data distribution (green) and projected data distribution (purple) [10]

should retain a lower value in order to declare sufficient performance. As illustrated in Fig. 5.6, the largest decrease in both ED and MMD values occurred after 32nd epoch. It is reasonable to suggest that the quality of the generated data is stabilized after this epoch.

Furthermore, the t-SNE [16] analysis is employed to assess how accurately the model perceives sensor readings' distribution. To this end, the distribution of both the original and projected ICS asset measurements is plotted in the two-dimensional space. In Fig. 5.7, one could observe the significant overlap between the original (blue color) and the perceived data (orange color), which indeed indicates that the proposed model was able to grasp the system behavior quite closely.

5.2.4 Cyber Incident Detection

The proposed method inferred 32 out of the 36 labeled attacks. A thorough comparison with the existing literature is presented in Table 5.2.

It is important to note that the dataset is intentionally kept as close as possible to the actual operational cycle so that the stabilization time was not eliminated from the test dataset as it was suggested in [2]. The stabilization period uncovers

Table 5.2 Performance across different anomaly detection methods. The results of DNN, SVM, DIF, MAD-GAN, and TABOT methods are taken from respective publications (rounded to the nearest hundredths)

Model	Precision	Recall	F-measure
DNN [5]	0.98	0.68	0.80
SVM [5]	0.93	0.70	0.80
DIF [2]	0.93	0.84	0.88
MAD-GAN [7]	0.99	0.64	0.77
TABOR [8]	0.86	0.79	0.82
This work	0.81	0.84	0.83

the impact of the attack on system operation and, thus, will contribute to cyber forensics' completeness. This discrepancy brings forth a higher number of false positives produced by the proposed approach, leading to a lower precision and F-measure. Thus, a direct comparison of the metric should only be made with this in mind.

The relative performance for each cyber incident is illustrated in Table 5.3, which compares the recall achieved by an offered method and that reported by different detection methods [10].

Please note that the dataset's attack scenarios consist of several attacks (5, 9, 12, 15, and 18) that do not affect physical properties and, thus, are irrelevant to this work. The table keeps the original scenario numbers while it excludes such attacks. The results of DNN, SVM, Dual-Isolation-Forest (DIF), and TABOR methods are taken from their respective publications and rounded to the nearest hundredths. The bold font in the table portrays the higher recall measure and validates that the proposed approach achieved a state-of-the-art comparative performance while surpassing available methods for several attacks.

5.2.5   Anomaly Localization

To reduce the computation load, the attribution method is employed for five ICS assets that display a higher reconstruction loss for each attack. Although the empirical evaluation is conducted for the investigation of each inferred attack, this section illustrates two representative examples and further compares the overall performance with prior works reported in the literature.

The inherent correlation of the elements in the water treatment ICS can cause false alarms using data-driven methods. Despite this false alarm, the introduced method outperformed competing algorithms for the single-point attack. Table 5.4 examines the attack attribution performance of our approach in contrast to those reported in [18] and [11].

Indeed, the presented method isolates more ICS assets affected by cyber incidents with fewer false alarms in contrast to those that were reported in the prior literature.

Table 5.3 Recall across different anomaly detection methods. The results of DNN, SVM, DIF, and TABOT methods are taken from their respective publications (rounded to the nearest hundredths)

Attack scenario	DNN [5]	SVM [5]	DIF [2]	TABOR [8]	This work
1	–	–	0.01	**0.05**	–
2	–	–	0.29	**0.93**	0.79
3	–	–	**1.00**	–	0.69
4	–	–	–	**0.33**	–
6	0.72	0.72	**1.00**	**1.00**	0.97
7	–	0.89	**1.00**	–	0.40
8	0.93	0.92	**1.00**	0.61	0.28
10	**1.00**	0.43	**1.00**	0.99	0.99
11	0.98	**1.00**	**1.00**	**1.00**	**1.00**
13	–	–	–	–	–
14	–	–	0.06	–	**0.35**
16	–	–	0.55	–	**0.91**
17	–	–	**0.64**	0.60	0.33
19	0.12	0.13	**0.45**	0.01	0.31
20	0.85	0.85	0.45	**1.00**	0.94
21	–	0.02	–	**0.08**	0.03
22	0.99	**1.00**	**1.00**	**1.00**	**1.00**
23	0.87	0.88	0.82	–	**0.99**
24	–	–	0.34	–	**0.39**
25	–	0.01	**1.00**	–	**1.00**
26	–	–	0.17	**1.00**	0.18
27	–	–	–	0.20	**0.97**
28	0.94	0.94	**1.00**	**1.00**	**1.00**
29	–	–	**1.00**	–	**1.00**
30	–	–	–	**1.00**	0.60
31	–	–	**1.00**	–	0.24
32	–	0.91	**1.00**	–	–
33	–	–	0.43	**0.89**	0.11
34	–	–	–	**0.99**	0.47
35	–	–	0.95	0.26	**1.00**
36	–	0.12	**0.93**	0.89	0.86
37	**1.00**	**1.00**	**1.00**	**1.00**	**1.00**
38	0.92	0.93	1.00	**1.00**	0.98
39	0.94	–	**1.00**	0.37	0.91
40	0.93	0.93	1.00	**1.00**	0.77
41	–	0.36	**0.63**	–	0.35

Table 5.4 A comparison of attack attribution across different methods

Model	Precision	Recall	F-measure
This work	**0.39**	**0.52**	**0.45**
Wang et al. [18]	0.30	0.43	0.35
Shalyga et al. [11]	0.22	0.21	0.21

Table 5.5 Attack scenarios considered in the case study

Ident.	Attack window	Attack duration	Description	Impact
16	11:57:25 AM–12:02:00 PM	04:35 min	An attacker gains control of the water level analyzer that measures the water level in the UF feed tank and decreases its level by 1 mm each second. The actual water level continues to increase, leading to tank overflow	Tank overflow
22	10:55:18 PM–11:03:00 PM	07:42 min	A regular operation cycle is as follows. Water from the reservation unit at process stage P4 moves to the process stage P5 via ultraviolet (UV) and cartridge filter. An attacker gains control of the three ICS assets at two different process levels: she sets the amount of water sensed by the analyzer as 150 and turns off the actuator. The false data forced PLC to stop one of the pumps at the purification process level	Physical damage

5.2.6   Interactive Visualization

Over further discussion, the case study considers the data related to two attack scenarios (Table 5.5) with their inference results. These two attack scenarios are selected to demonstrate the examples for which the proposed approach *(i)* shows equivalent performance as [2, 5, 8], and *(ii)* outperforms the respective literature.

The result of the attack inference module is passed to the anomaly attribution module as a set of measurements indicating the probability that the system is exploited at a particular time point. As the attribution algorithm allows a combination of several methods, for validation purposes, the experiment selected the following feature importance techniques: Classification and Regression Trees (CARTs) [1], Logistic Regression [6], and Shapley values [12].

Table 5.6 provides a deeper look at the classification of the attack rendered by the detection engine.

This classification, however, presents several discrepancies with the attack log. For instance, in scenario 16, an attack log indicates only level indicator LIT301 as exploited, rendering the original attack class SSSP. Due to the adverse effect of the attack on the water level in the tank in the subsequent process level, the

Table 5.6 Deeper look into considered attack scenarios

Ident.	Process	Exploited assets	Attack type
16[a]	P1, P3	LIT301, LIT101	MSMP
22	P4, P5	UV401, AIT502, P501	MSMP

[a] An attack log indicates only level indicator LIT301 as exploited, rendering the original attack class SSSP. The discrepancy has occurred due to the adverse effect of the attack on the water level in the tank

Table 5.7 The result of anomaly localization for attack scenario 16. Bold font indicates the correctly identified ICS assets

Model	Reported affected ICS assets
This work	**LIT301**, LIT101
Wang et al. [18]	–
Shalyga et al. [11]	MV301, MV303

Table 5.8 The result of anomaly localization for attack scenario 22. Bold font indicates the correctly identified ICS assets

Model	Reported affected ICS assets
This work	**UV401, AIT502, P501**
Wang et al. [18]	**UV401, P501**, FIT504
Shalyga et al. [11]	DPIT301, MV302

proposed anomaly attribution algorithm denotes level indicator LIT101 as affected by a cyber incident. In particular, the introduced method assigned a score for LIT101 into 83rd percentile. In contrast, the score for the correctly pinpointed level indicator LIT301 falls into the 100th percentile. A comparison with state of the art (Table 5.7) demonstrates the better precision of the introduced localization method.

In scenario 22, the incident log registered the following affected points: valve UV401, water level indicator AIT501, and pump P501. As noted in Table 5.8, the introduced algorithm correctly identifies affected ICS assets and outperforms the previously proposed methods.

The final result of the attack inference and attribution module is passed to a visual analytics component in the form of JSON files. Concurrently, the visualization module receives resilience indices to convert them into visual representation to focus the attention of the domain expert.

In order to support the investigation of the potential progress of the cyber incident, a Pearson correlation for each ICS asset is calculated and plotted (Fig. 5.8.) The results are further used in the *inspection view*.

In the visual module, the domain expert employs the analytical strategies by navigating through the coordinated views and by configuring parameters (detection model, critical assets, thresholds) as needed.

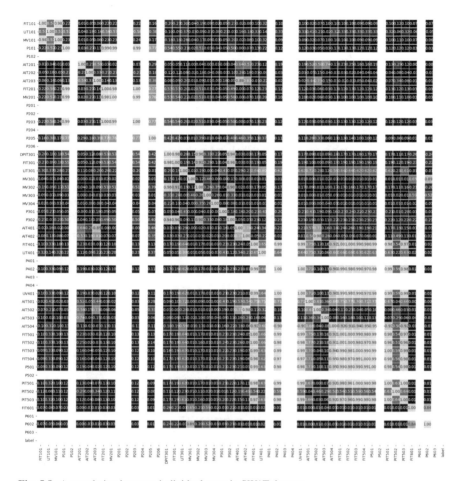

Fig. 5.8 A correlation between individual asset in SWAT dataset

Incident 16

Figure 5.9 illustrates a detailed view for the detected attack scenario 16. An attacker gains control of the water level analyzer that measures the water level in the UF feed tank and decreases its level by 1 mm each second. The actual water level continues to increase, leading to tank overflow. The *inspection view* reflected this attack and pinpointed that the critical asset defined in the settings is exploited.

Incident 22

The inference mechanism precisely isolates the incident by assigning a high irregularity score. Interestingly, the attack's start is 22 seconds earlier than recorded in the attack log. The manual investigation confirmed that the dataset labeled an attack with this specific delay. In addition, the dataset marks recovery time as a regular operation; however, it is essential to infer a stabilization period for further

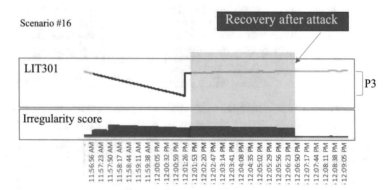

Fig. 5.9 An example of sensor measurements and actuators' states during an attack (red) and their inference. The red color indicates an attack window [10]

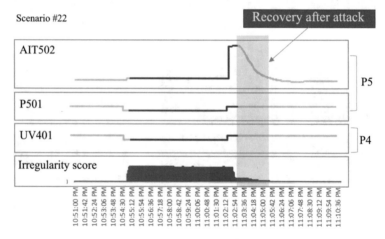

Fig. 5.10 An example of sensor measurements and actuators' states during an attack (red) and their inference. The red color indicates an attack window [10]

investigation of a potential impact on the system since it may take a long time (sometimes hours) for ICS to return to regular operation. These discrepancies lead to false positives produced by the inference method at the beginning and after the attack (Fig. 5.10).

In this scenario, an attacker sets the amount of water sensed by the analyzer as 150 and turns off the actuator. The false data forced PLC to stop one of the pumps at the purification process level.

Taking investigation further, the *raw data view* visually compares the actual measurements of the ICS asset with the expected data points. The behavior of AIT502 shows a significant apparent deviation from the expected one and indicates the accuracy of the anomaly attribution mechanism.

5.3 Summary

Aiming to support cyber forensics in the context of ICS deployed in smart cities, this chapter introduces an unsupervised approach that infers cyber-attacks and reveals the attacked assets for forensics' prioritization. The model is strengthened by BiGAN, RNN, CNN, and Shapley values of residual error. The former component is advantageous for learning underlying data in-depth. RNN is valuable for time series processing, while CNN can learn features and extract patterns. Finally, Shapley values provide the ability to trace the potential attack points from both class-wise and model-wise perspectives.

The approach has three distinguishing characteristics: *(i)* it operates with multivariate data, which is highly desired in ICS deployed in water treatment plants, *(ii)* it is trained using only attack-free instances and therefore can avoid the problem of imbalanced data, *(iii)* it identifies the attack points and thus can reduce forensics' overhead in critical infrastructure realms.

The effectiveness of the proposed approach is demonstrated by employing it to data collected by a testbed representing a small-scale water treatment plant. Most of the attacks presented in the empirical data were detected with high sensitivity, while the inference method maintained a high irregularity score after the threat has passed. The latter is affected by the time system required for recovery after an attack. The results of the empirical evaluations demonstrate the capability of the proposed approach to infer and attribute the attacks with equivalent or better performance over state-of-the-art methods.

The detection of cyber-attacks against ICS is a complex task that can rarely be solved using only automatic data mining methods. Numerous methods rely on anomaly detection as a technique to discover attacks against ICS. Cybersecurity and forensics analysts face several challenges when exploring the massive number of records generated by a large number of heterogeneous ISC assets.

This chapter introduced visual analytics that supports the analysis of inferred anomaly and enables the domain expert to decide whether it represents a false alarm or looks for more information if it is impossible to reach a confident conclusion. To achieve this, the method first designs model domain-aware analytical reasoning and then maps it to the appropriate visual techniques, views, and appropriate interaction. The proposed approach offers several benefits. It makes the attacks visible; therefore, it can reduce the cybersecurity analysts' and forensics investigators' operational overhead. It helps quickly identify exploited ICS assets for targeted investigation, facilitating remediation and forensics prioritization. Besides, it allows examination from diverse perspectives and supports the top-down analysis. It retains the presentation of findings to other investigators or interested parties.

References

1. Leo Breiman, Jerome Friedman, Charles J Stone, and Richard A Olshen. *Classification and regression trees*. CRC press, 1984.
2. M. Elnour, N. Meskin, K. Khan, and R. Jain. A Dual-Isolation-Forests-Based Attack Detection Framework for Industrial Control Systems. *IEEE Access*, 8:36639–36651, 2020.
3. Jonathan Goh, Sridhar Adepu, Khurum Nazir Junejo, and Aditya Mathur. A dataset to support research in the design of secure water treatment systems. In *International Conference on Critical Information Infrastructures Security*, pages 88–99. Springer, 2016.
4. Amin Hassanzadeh, Amin Rasekh, Stefano Galelli, Mohsen Aghashahi, Riccardo Taormina, Avi Ostfeld, and M Katherine Banks. A review of cybersecurity incidents in the water sector. *Journal of Environmental Engineering*, 146(5):03120003, 2020.
5. Jun Inoue, Yoriyuki Yamagata, Yuqi Chen, Christopher M Poskitt, and Jun Sun. Anomaly detection for a water treatment system using unsupervised machine learning. In *2017 IEEE international conference on data mining workshops (ICDMW)*, pages 1058–1065. IEEE, 2017.
6. David G Kleinbaum, K Dietz, M Gail, Mitchel Klein, and Mitchell Klein. *Logistic regression*. Springer, 2002.
7. Dan Li, Dacheng Chen, Baihong Jin, Lei Shi, Jonathan Goh, and See-Kiong Ng. MAD-GAN: Multivariate anomaly detection for time series data with generative adversarial networks. In *International Conference on Artificial Neural Networks*, pages 703–716. Springer, 2019.
8. Qin Lin, Sridha Adepu, Sicco Verwer, and Aditya Mathur. TABOR: A graphical model-based approach for anomaly detection in industrial control systems. In *Proceedings of the 2018 on Asia Conference on Computer and Communications Security*, pages 525–536, 2018.
9. A. P. Mathur and N. O. Tippenhauer. SWaT: a water treatment testbed for research and training on ICS security. In *2016 International Workshop on Cyber-physical Systems for Smart Water Networks (CySWater)*, pages 31–36, April 2016.
10. Nataliia Neshenko, Elias Bou-Harb, and Borko Furht. A Behavioral-based Forensic Investigation Approach for Analyzing Attacks on Water Plants Using GANs. *Forensic Science International: Digital Investigation*, 2021.
11. Dmitry Shalyga, Pavel Filonov, and Andrey Lavrentyev. Anomaly detection for water treatment system based on neural network with automatic architecture optimization. *arXiv preprint arXiv:1807.07282*, 2018.
12. Lloyd S Shapley. A value for n-person games. *Contributions to the Theory of Games*, 2(28):307–317, 1953.
13. Esther Shein. Incident of the week: Cyber criminals launch ransomware attack on water utility in hurricane ravaged n.c., Oct 2018.
14. TOI staff, Amy Spiro, Tobias Siegal, Tobias Siegal staff, TOI, Lazar Berman, Lazar Berman Keller-Lynn, Carrie, TOI staff Keller-Lynn, Carrie, Amy Spiro, Jamey Keaten, TOI staff Agencies, , and et al. Cyber attacks again hit Israel's water system, shutting agricultural pumps, Jul 2020.
15. Gábor J Székely and Maria L Rizzo. Energy statistics: A class of statistics based on distances. *Journal of statistical planning and inference*, 143(8):1249–1272, 2013. Publisher: Elsevier.
16. Laurens Van der Maaten and Geoffrey Hinton. Visualizing data using t-SNE. *Journal of machine learning research*, 9(11), 2008.

17. B Verizon. Data breach digest. scenarios from the field, 2016.
18. Chao Wang, Bailing Wang, Hongri Liu, and Haikuo Qu. Anomaly Detection for Industrial Control System Based on Autoencoder Neural Network. *Wireless Communications and Mobile Computing*, 2020, 2020. Publisher: Hindawi.
19. Onslow Water and Sewer Authority | Official Website. Onslow water and sewer authority: Official website.

Chapter 6
Looking Ahead: Future Perspectives and Opportunities of Cyber Situational Awareness for Smart Cities

Cyber threats and attacks induced by exploiting advanced heterogeneous technologies to target smart cities worldwide are evolving rapidly. Thus, failing to control these cyber threats undermines the trustworthiness of the transformational projects that aim at making cities more sustainable and livable for their citizens. From a literature survey of the topics related to cyber situational awareness in the context of smart cities (Chap. 3), it is evident that this imperative task seems to be in a juvenile stage. Although research and operational communities are actively developing the methods to address this imperative task, numerous observations require attention. This chapter encapsulates several issues on sustained cyber situational awareness for smart cities and elaborates on several possible research directions to address these topics.

6.1 Challenges and Future Perspective

This section outlines a number of research and operational challenges (Fig. 6.1). It pinpoints several initiatives (both technical and non-technical) for future work, which are worthy of being pursued to support sustainable situational awareness for smart cities [2].

The Lack of Holistic Framework for Situational Awareness
Cyber situational awareness is a complex task that requires a holistic and systematic approach. To this end, Chap. 4 of this book defines the activities needed to enforce a situational awareness program and elaborates on design challenges that hinder the transition to operation in smart city realms.

Additionally, there seems to be no holistic solution to address the prioritization threat in the context of specific infrastructure (e.g., energy, transportation, health, etc.). To this end, Chap. 4 of this book makes a step toward this imperative task by introducing a framework for situational awareness for Industrial Control Systems

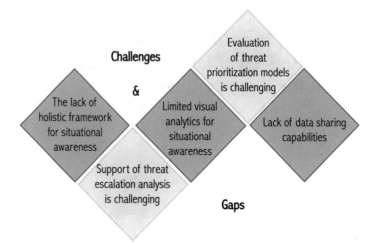

Fig. 6.1 Challenges for the development of sustained cyber situational awareness for smart cities

(ICSs), and Chap. 5 presents the application of this framework in the particular case of the water treatment plant.

Moreover, the operational community would benefit from the attack trend analysis to develop targeted and more effective remediation strategies, including those related to the specific devices' vendors.

Finally, the current literature mostly focuses on attack detection in the realm of one smart city component, omitting to model the dependencies among various critical infrastructures. The relationships are not always straightforward: a complex interdependence between individual entities in critical infrastructure plays a significant role in the development of smart cities [4]. However, it seems that many available models are unable to capture such complex interdependency to grasp the full array of intentional and accidental threats. On the other hand, it is crucial to frame identified threats and detected cyber incidents in the context of smart cities' operations and comprehend their real impact on mission-critical services. The development of a complete solution requires interdisciplinary research.

Support of Threat Escalation Analysis Is Challenging

It is imperative to acknowledge the need for a proactive approach to secure a smart city at various architectural levels. Additionally, given a shortage in the security-related budget, effective resource allocation is one of the requirements for extending the cyber resilience of the smart city. Threat escalation approaches should be thoroughly investigated to support cyber decisions. To this end, Chap. 4 introduces the framework that opens a conversation regarding this matter.

There is a road ahead, however. Several solutions could help with prioritizing decisions. The first possible extension is providing the information regarding the time required for the investigation and the remediation of detected malicious events.

Second, the effectiveness of previously applied defense mechanisms to a similar problem should be thoroughly investigated and reported. Third, the cost-benefit analysis of mitigation strategies can trigger a conversation toward effective cyber security investments. In this context, more research can be pursued to support the decision-making process for smart cities' security.

Limited Visual Analytics for Situational Awareness
One of the biggest challenges of situational awareness is the amount and quality of information that should be analyzed. Although automated methods rooted in machine learning and the computational power of modern computers enable effective data processing, the analysis still requires human judgment in order to make the best possible evaluation of the result and eliminate the negative effect of conflicting or incomplete data. In this context, visual analytics connects computational data analysis methods and human reasoning in the decision-making process through visualization and interaction. Such integration, known as visual analytics, is largely perceived by the research community [3]. In particular, it synthesizes information to derive insights and communicate the assessment for a prompt response.

However, the usage of human cognition to identify and track threats' progress, evaluate supporting information, and enhance decision-making seems to be in its infancy in the context of smart city cyber situational awareness. Surprisingly, a limited amount of studied works made an attempt to visualize the results, even though it can allow cyber analysts to accomplish their responsibilities with more extensive support. Without such capabilities, the practical implementation of the analytical models is problematic, especially since smart cities have such a complex environment.

Evaluation of Threat Prioritization Models Is Challenging
Another significant challenge of threat exploration methods in smart city settings is their evaluation. Indeed, limited visibility of dependencies between components in the entire ecosystem, continually evolving threats, and the lack of visibility into past cyber security incidents make it challenging to establish ground truth. Additionally, most of the reviewed methods validated the results through generic, illustrative scenarios.

However, the lack of connection with real-world applications questions the validity of the evaluated approaches. Moreover, the reliability of the proposed methods is also rarely measured because of the broad lack of empirical data (for comparisons). Therefore, the application of field strategies such as interviews, experiments, and similar studies can be instrumental in addressing the evaluation task. For the visual analytics community, it could symbolize the creation of visual techniques to reveal the insights of machine learning models or to create a visual representation of threats progression through the entire system of smart cities.

Lack of Data Sharing Capabilities
Despite advances in the field of cyber security and cyber situational awareness, in particular, the main challenge of generalizing knowledge derived from the limited

collection of previously inferred malicious events related to smart cities remains unsolved. Due to the lack of publicly available raw data regarding events and their impact on various aspects of smart cities, the models are evaluated based on the data generated in laboratory setups. However, the datasets play a vital role in validating the approaches. To increase awareness and facilitate joint efforts for the prevention of cyber-attacks, the U.S. Congress recently passed the Cyber Incident Reporting for Critical Infrastructure Act of 2022 (CIRCIA) [1]. It requires critical infrastructure organizations, which include financial, energy companies, and other key businesses for which a disruption would impact economic security or public health and safety, to report substantial cybersecurity incidents or ransom payments to the federal government.

Additionally, it appears that the studied methods enumerate threats and attacks manually, without formal representation, not to mention the absence of sharing capabilities. Moreover, generating, maintaining, and sharing the knowledge base regarding attack plans can be a possible solution to this issue. Furthermore, with the increasing number of malicious incidents, the systematic approach of collecting, indexing, and correlating incidents enables comprehensive situational awareness, faster detection, and mitigation. Therefore, establishing relevant datasets with a sufficient amount of data, broad scope, and an even number of attack types can support the solution of the evaluation problem and improve the threat scope. Additionally, while considering the ethical aspect, sharing raw data is a candidate for a possible solution to this issue. Another aspect to consider herein is the peculiarities of ICS deployed in smart cities. Various ICS have different operating goals, even if they are deployed within the same industry's boundaries. Examples include but are not limited to water treatment and its distribution. Therefore, the choice of empirical data may influence the result. For instance, water distribution systems are prone to pattern instability (e.g., water consumption). To this end, the methods should be evaluated using different empirical data collections to advance the capabilities of the methods.

6.2 Summary

Cyber situational awareness for smart cities is a critical task for their survival. Given the mounting number of cyber-attacks and their impact on the safety of city residents and on the legacy infrastructure, their corresponding financial concerns require new kinds of situational awareness in order to overcome their resultant implications. Although research and operating communities approach this crucial task by introducing new methods rooted in empirical data and advanced analytics, there is a long road ahead. This chapter showcased significant research gaps that emerged from the literature review and pinpointed the importance of a holistic approach to cyber situational awareness in the context of smart cities.

References

1. Eversheds Sutherland (US) LLP. The cyber incident reporting for critical infrastructure act of 2022. https://www.jdsupra.com/legalnews/the-cyber-incident-reporting-for-6058324/. Accessed: 2022-05-09.
2. Nataliia Neshenko, Christelle Nader, Elias Bou-Harb, and Borko Furht. A survey of methods supporting cyber situational awareness in the context of smart cities. *Journal of Big Data*, 7(1):1–41, 2020. Publisher: SpringerOpen.
3. James J Thomas and Kristin A Cook. A visual analytics agenda. *IEEE computer graphics and applications*, 26(1):10–13, 2006.
4. Inger Anne Tøndel, Jørn Foros, Stine Skaufel Kilskar, Per Hokstad, and Martin Gilje Jaatun. Interdependencies and reliability in the combined ICT and power system: An overview of current research. *Applied computing and informatics*, 14(1):17–27, 2018.

Printed in the United States
by Baker & Taylor Publisher Services